The Making of a Vision

"I was not disobedient to the heavenly vision."
(Acts 26:19)

Frank Damazio

© *City Bible Publishing* • 9200 NE Fremont • Portland, Oregon 97220

Published by City Bible Publishing
9200 NE Fremont
Portland, Oregon 97220

Printed in U.S.A.

City Bible Publishing is a ministry of City Bible Church and is dedicated to serving the local church and its leaders through the production and distribution of quality restoration materials.

It is our prayer that these materials, proven in the context of the local church, will equip leaders in exalting the Lord and extending His kingdom.

For a free catalog of additional resources from City Bible Publishing please call 1-800-777-6057 or visit our web site at www.citybiblepublishing.com.

The Making of a Vision – Student Handbook
© Copyright 2002 by City Bible Publishing
All Rights Reserved

ISBN 1-886849-90-0

The Making of a Vision

Introduction to Vision

I. THE NEED OF VISION

A. Proverbs 29:18
1. "Where there is no vision, the people perish." (KJV)
2. "Where there is no vision, the people are made naked." (KJV margin)
3. "Where there is no vision (no redemptive revelations of God), the people perish." (Amplified Old Testament)
4. "Where there is no vision (revelation), the people are unrestrained." (NASB)
5. "Where there is no revelation, the people cast off restraint." (NIV)
6. "Without prophecy, the people become demoralized." (NAB)
7. "Where there is no progressive vision, the people dwell carelessly." (Swedish)
8. "Where there are no guidelines, the people run riot."
9. "Where there is no word from God, the people are uncontrolled."
10. "Where there is ignorance of God, the people run wild." (LD)
11. "Without revelation a nation fades, but it prospers in knowing the law." (FF)
12. "Where there is no vision, the people cast off restraint." (JND)

B. The absolute need of vision. The above conditions are the results in a church or an individual who lacks vision. Vision gives direction; vision gives motivation. Without vision there is no direction and no motivation. People perish; churches perish. People do not want to follow someone or something that is perishing.

II. GREAT LACK IN MOST LEADERSHIP TRAINING

A. Most seminaries and Christian colleges do not teach vision in their basic educational structure.

B. Most theological books leave vision out completely or they treat it superficially.

C. Most Christian organizations and churches have been built by gifted leaders with vision rather than by a shared vision of both the leadership team and the congregation

III. GREAT CHALLENGE FOR 21ST CENTURY LEADERSHIP

A. The challenge of grasping, processing, establishing, guarding and implementing a balanced vision.

B. The challenge of understanding the times culturally, spiritually and prophetically.

C. The challenge of adapting a right leadership style in accomplishing a successful vision.

IV. GREAT GOALS OF THIS MATERIAL

A.   To thoroughly understand the meaning of a biblically based vision that is built on the eternal purposes of God.

B.   To encourage all leaders to become visionary leaders that grasp God's vision and empower others to fulfill vision.

C.   To establish a clear process to enable leaders to know their spiritual capacity, gifting and leadership style.

D.   To educate the leader with spiritual wisdom that discerns the destroyers of vision and how to overcome these vision obstacles.

E.   To help the leader learn the process in making a vision statement with the opportunity to view many other vision statements.

F.   To instruct the visionary leader in the fine art of vision implementation.

Vision in Scripture

Gen 15:1 the LORD came unto Abram in a *vision*
Gen 46:2 unto Israel in the *vision*s of the night
Num 12:6 make myself known unto him in a *vision*
Num 24:4 which saw the *vision* of the Almighty
Num 24:16 which saw the *vision* of the Almighty
1 Sam 3:1 there was no open *vision*
1 Sam 3:15 Samuel feared to shew Eli the *vision*
2 Sam 7:17 and according to all this *vision*
1 Chr 17:15 and according to all this *vision*
2 Chr 32:32 written in the *vision* of Isaiah
Job 20:8 chased away as a *vision* of the night
Job 33:15 in a *vision* of the night, when deep
Ps 89:19 thou spakest in *vision* to thy holy one
Prov 29:18 Where there is no *vision*
Isaiah 1:1 The *vision* of Isaiah the son of Amoz
Isaiah 21:2 A grievous *vision* is declared unto me
Isaiah 22:1 The burden of the valley of *vision*
Isaiah 22:5 GOD of hosts in the valley of *vision*
Isaiah 28:7 they err in *vision*, they stumble in
Isaiah 29:7 shall be as a dream of a night *vision*
Isaiah 29:11 And the *vision* of all is become
Jer 14:14 they prophesy unto you a false *vision*
Jer 23:16 they speak a *vision* of their own heart
Lam 2:9 also find no *vision* from the LORD
Ezek 7:13 for the *vision* is touching the whole
Ezek 7:26 they seek a *vision* of the prophet
Ezek 8:4 according to the *vision* that I saw in
Ezek 11:24 brought me in a *vision* by the Spirit
Ezek 11:24 so the *vision* that I had seen went up
Ezek 12:22 are prolonged, and every *vision* faileth
Ezek 12:23 at hand, and the effect of every *vision*
Ezek 12:24 vain *vision* nor flattering divination
Ezek 12:27 the *vision* that he seeth is for many
Ezek 13:7 Have ye not seen a vain *vision*
Ezek 43:3 appearance of the *vision* which I saw
Daniel 2:19 revealed unto Daniel in a night *vision*
Daniel 7:2 and said, I saw in my *vision* by night
Daniel 8:1 a *vision* appeared unto me
Daniel 8:2 and I saw in a *vision*
Daniel 8:2 and I saw in a *vision*, and I was by
Daniel 8:13 how long shall be the *vision*
Daniel 8:15 I, even I Daniel, had seen the *vision*
Daniel 8:16 make this man to understand the *vision*
Daniel 8:17 time of the end shall be the *vision*
Daniel 8:26 the *vision* of the evening and the
Daniel 8:26 wherefore shut thou up the *vision*
Daniel 8:27 and I was astonished at the *vision*
Daniel 9:21 seen in the *vision* at the beginning
Daniel 9:23 the matter, and consider the *vision*
Daniel 9:24 and to seal up the *vision* and prophecy
Daniel 10:1 and had understanding of the *vision*
Daniel 10:7 And I Daniel alone saw the *vision*
Daniel 10:8 left alone, and saw this great *vision*

Daniel 10:14 for yet the *vision* is for many days
Daniel 10:16 by the *vision* my sorrows are turned
Daniel 11:14 themselves to establish the *vision*
Obad 1:1 The *vision* of Obadiah
Micah 3:6 you, that ye shall not have a *vision*
Nahum 1:1 The book of the *vision* of Nahum the
Hab 2:2 and said, Write the *vision*
Hab 2:3 For the *vision* is yet for an appointed time
Zech 13:4 be ashamed every one of his *vision*
Matt 17:9 Tell the *vision* to no man, until the
Luke 1:22 he had seen a *vision* in the temple
Luke 24:23 they had also seen a *vision* of angels
Acts 9:10 and to him said the Lord in a *vision*
Acts 9:12 hath seen in a *vision* a man named
Acts 10:3 He saw in a *vision* evidently about the
Acts 10:17 doubted in himself what this *vision*
Acts 10:19 While Peter thought on the *vision*
Acts 11:5 and in a trance I saw a *vision*
Acts 12:9 but thought he saw a *vision*
Acts 16:9 a *vision* appeared to Paul in the night
Acts 16:10 And after he had seen the *vision*
Acts 18:9 Lord to Paul in the night by a *vision*
Acts 26:19 disobedient unto the heavenly *vision*
Rev 9:17 And thus I saw the horses in the *vision*
2 Chr 9:29 in the *vision*s of Iddo the seer against
2 Chr 26:5 had understanding in the *vision*s of God
Job 4:13 thoughts from the *vision*s of the night
Job 7:14 and terrifiest me through *vision*s
Ezek 1:1 were opened, and I saw *vision*s of God
Ezek 8:3 brought me in the *vision*s of God to
Ezek 13:16 which see *vision*s of peace for her
Ezek 40:2 In the *vision*s of God brought he me
Ezek 43:3 the *vision*s were like the *vision* that I
Daniel 1:17 Daniel had understanding in all *vision*s
Daniel 2:28 the *vision*s of thy head upon thy bed
Daniel 4:5 the *vision*s of my head troubled me
Daniel 4:9 tell me the *vision*s of my dream that I
Daniel 4:10 Thus were the *vision*s of mine head in
Daniel 4:13 I saw in the *vision*s of my head upon my
Daniel 7:1 *vision*s of his head upon his bed
Daniel 7:7 After this I saw in the night *vision*s
Daniel 7:13 I saw in the night *vision*s, and, behold
Daniel 7:15 the *vision*s of my head troubled me
Hosea 12:10 prophets, and I have multiplied *vision*s
Joel 2:28 your young men shall see *vision*s
Acts 2:17 your young men shall see *vision*s
2 Cor 12:1 I will come to *vision*s and revelations

The Trilogy of Vision Fulfillment

THEOLOGY Foundation for Vision	TEACHING Formation of Vision	TEAMWORK Fulfillment of Vision
1. Theology of the Purpose of God	Understanding the Biblical Vision	The Visionary Leader
2. Theology of the Church	Strategy in Establishing Vision	The Church in the City
3. Theology of the Body of Christ	Principles of Vision Advancement	The Networking Church
4. Theology of Five-fold Ministry	Discerning Vision Destroyers	The Equipping Church
5. Theology of Church Leadership	Diagnosis of 21st Century Culture	The Lay Ministry-Driven Church
6. Theology of Christian Maturity	The Momentum Mystery	The Discipling Church
7. Theology of Pastoral Ministry	The Warfare of Vision	The Timothy Training Church
8. Theology of the Gospel Message	The Resources of Vision	The Harvesting Church
9. Theology of the Holy Spirit	Expanding Vision Through Faith	The Gifts Functioning Church
10. Theology of God	Growing Vision Through Principles	The Presence of God Church
11. Theology of Preaching	Imparting Vision Through Preaching	The Feeding of the Word Church
12. Theology of the Kingdom	Implementation of Vision	The Building Character Church

6

Cultivating a Vision for Your Life

Every church must have a vision, clear, distinct, focused, calling the church to be and to do. Yet corporate vision is tied to the personal vision of the catalytic leader at the helm! The developing of a personal vision is foundational to developing a ministry vision and a church vision. The same disciplines of prayer, dedication, and preciseness are used in both the personal and the corporate vision development.

> "Few words are bandied about and misunderstood as much as the word vision. For some people, it means jotting down a few lofty goals once a year and then experience that transcends everyday experience. Both miss the mark. A vision is a guiding light to live by, 365 days a year. It is the reason you go to work and the reason your organization exists. A real vision gets tucked away in the mind; not the drawer; it shapes every thought and decision. At the same time, a vision is a spiritual statement of one's relation to God and the rest of humanity. It is this very quality that makes it so relevant to our day-to-day experience; a true vision is a blueprint for daily action."
>
> (K. Blanchard, Forward to <u>Vision Driven Leadership</u>)

I Samuel 3:1; Hosea 12:10; Joel 2:28; Acts 2:17; Acts 9:10-12; Acts 16:9-10; Acts 18:9; Acts 26:19

Having a personal vision means discerning God's will for our lives and ministry. This vision is based upon present and past experiences plus understanding of what God desires to do in the future.

I. PERSONAL VISION BEGINS WITH SERIOUS EVALUATION

    A. Honest Evaluation – Hard Questions
    (Ephesians 5:15-16)

        1. Where am I?

        2. Where am I going?

FORMATIVE YEARS   STRETCHING YEARS   SETTLING YEARS

3.   What are my strengths and weaknesses?

4.   What are my dreams?

5.   What are my realistic goals?

6.   What is it you feel God has for your life?

7.   What specifically would your function be in the Body of Christ?

8.   What are some of your inner dreams and hopes? How can these hidden ambitions become realities?

B.   Potential Personal Obstacles
1.   I don't have what it takes.
2.   I don't have the motivation.
3.   I don't have the training.
4.   I don't have the self-discipline.
5.   I don't want the responsibility.
6.   I lack the energy.
7.   I'm not a self-starter.
8.   I'm too old/young.
9.   I don't have the time.
10.   I don't have the money.

II. THE SEVEN BIBLICAL FACTORS THAT BUILD PERSONAL VISION
(Romans 8:26-30)

A.   The Holy Spirit knows and supports you in your present limitations
(Romans 8:26)

B.   The Holy Spirit intercedes for you because of your limited vision
(Romans 8:26-27)

C.   The divine mystery that God causes all things to work together for good
(Romans 8:28)

D.   God has perfect knowledge of your past, present and future
(II Corinthians 12:9-10; Romans 8:29; 11:2; II Peter 3:17; Acts 2:23; I Peter 1:12)

E.   God has already set boundary lines for my life and for my good
     (Romans 8:29-30; Acts 4:28; I Corinthians 2:7; Ephesians 1:5,11)

F.   God has given me an invitation to fulfill my destiny
     (Rom 8:30; Isaiah 41:9; I Corinth 15:9; Gal 1:15; Heb 11:8; I Tim 6:12; Rev 19:9)

G.   God has provided for me a new identity based on his work
     (Romans 8:30; 4:5; 5:1; Galatians 2:16; Romans 3:30; 5:9)

III.   CULTIVATING PERSONAL VISION WITH A PRACTICAL PLAN

A.   The Five Step Plan

1.   Desire

2.   Visualization

3.   Association

4.   Concentration

5.   Imagination

B.   Practical Necessary Steps

1.   Write out your purpose in life and your dreams.

2.   Pray and fast to receive God's assurance.

3.   Communicate it to those you respect.

4.   Begin to set new priorities that complement your vision.

5.   Begin to forget past failures and take some faith steps.

IV. COUNTING THE COST OF PERSONAL VISION

A. Scriptures – Luke 14:25-33; Proverbs 6:6-11; 30:25; Ecclesiastes 2:18-23; 10:18

B. The Cost Analysis

1. To consider one's goals and purpose in a realistic way.

2. To calculate how much energy and effort is needed to accomplish the whole task.

3. To anticipate distractions, hindrances, snares and traps that will be in your path.

4. To list all the privileges you enjoy and then determine by careful analysis if these privileges will weaken your progression toward your goals. If they do, you must lay them aside.

5. To make a covenant with yourself that you will not give up in times of great discouragement, frustration or pressure.

6. To unite yourself with the kind of people who are going in the same direction.

7. To purpose in your spirit that you will accomplish God's purpose for your life in God's timing and in God's way.

V. PERSONAL VISION CULTIVATED WITH DREAMS AND GOALS
(Proverbs 24:3)

A. Dreams Determine My Course
(Proverbs 13:12)

1. To dream is to anticipate that which is to come to pass and contemplate it with pleasure.

2. To dream is to have a fond hope and aspiration for the future.

3. To dream is to be totally overtaken by a desire that motivates you toward your destiny.

4. To dream is to face every obstacle with the determination of a winner.

5. To dream is to set specific goals to mark achievement by.

B.   A Course Charted by Goals

    1.   Goal: A point toward which effort or movement is directed, the object point in which one is trying to reach. Something that lies in the future. Statements about what could be, what should be and what can be.

    2.   Necessity of Goals
        a.   It is realistic goals that you set for yourself that make life interesting, meaningful and exciting.
        b.   Without goals we have nothing to measure our effort by.
        c.   Without goals man becomes purposeless and life becomes unimportant.
        d.   Without goals we have nothing to confess in faith about.
        e.   Without goals or vision, people perish (Proverbs 29:18)
        f.   Without purpose and goals man becomes a wandering bird, which is the spirit of your day.
        g.   Without purpose and goals is to be without motivation.

VI.   THE OBSTACLES OF PERSONAL VISION

A.   The Helmsman
    1.   James 3:4 "Lo, the ship also being of such proportions and driven by hard winds, being steered by the least rudder, wherever the impulse of the helmsman is intending."
    2.   Definition: "The place or post of direction or management, place of orders, the ship is directed by his knowledge of the course chartered."

B.   Obstacles

    1.   Your Own Self

    2.   Your Past

    3.   Your Resources

    4.   Your Frame of Reference

    5.   The 3-D Obstacle
        a.   Disappointment
        b.   Discouragement
        c.   Delays

VII. THE FULFILLMENT OF PERSONAL VISION
(II Timothy 4:7)

A. Keeping the Vision Alive

> *Great is it to believe in a dream,*
> *When you stand in life by a stormy stream.*
> *But greater is it to live life through*
> *And say in the end "The dream was true."*

B. Protecting the Vision

　　1. The Demas Trap
　　　　(II Timothy 4:10)

　　2. The John Mark Testimony
　　　　(II Timothy 4:11)

　　3. The Paul Triumph
　　　　(II Timothy 4:5-9)

A Prayer for Fulfilling Personal Vision

I surrender my life into the hands of God, knowing He has predestined for me His best. I will count the cost and, by God's grace, pay the price to become the best I am capable of becoming. I will hold to my course and by the power of the Holy Spirit finish strong!

Cultivating a Vision for Your Mission

Commissioned. What comes to your mind? The future belongs to those who have a sense of being commissioned by God. Commissioned people are those who truly live life with an attitude of "I can make a difference." My desire is to inspire every person to reach out and grasp the specific mission God has given you. Your mission in life will affect those within your immediate surroundings. Your mission will cause you to become a person of responsibility and influence in your local church, your local community and ultimately in your world. Come discover your mission and answer some questions like: What would you do with your life if you knew it was impossible to fail? Am I making a difference in my world of living? Do I have a sense of destiny and mission? (Ephesians 5:15-16)

I. THREE DIMENSIONS OF MISSION THAT DIRECT MINISTRY DEVELOPMENT

A. *The Eternal/Divine Dimension of Mission*
The mission God has established is called His eternal purpose. This purpose is evident in the restored New Testament church, reconciling people to Christ and restoring their lives to proper working order, in harmony with His design. (Genesis 1:26-28; Ephesians 3:10-11)

B. *The Local Church Time/Space Dimension of Mission*
Each generation must pursue and establish God's mission within their sphere of influence in their culture, their geographical area and discern their specific part to fulfill while moving in harmony with the whole. (Acts 2:27-37; Matthew 16:16-18)

C. *The Individualized/Personalized Dimension of Mission*
The effective believer is one who has laid hold of one mastering, divine mission for his or her life, mastering it through discipline, focus, sacrifice, prayer and fasting, thus becoming a mission-minded achiever. (Phil 3:13-14; Acts 13:36)

II. IDENTIFYING PERSONAL MISSION AND DESTINY
"The poorest man is not he who is without a cent, but he who is without a dream!"

A.   Vision shaped the destiny of Noah
(Genesis 6-7; Hebrews 11:7)

B.   Vision shaped the destiny of Abraham
(Genesis 11-22; Hebrews 11:8-11)

C.   Vision shaped the destiny of Moses
        (Exodus 1-6; Hebrews 11:23-27)

D.   Vision shaped the destiny of Nehemiah
        (Nehemiah 1:1-5)

III.   MISSION: THE FOUNDATION TO MINISTRY

A.   Com-Mission

        1.   "Com" = from the old Latin meaning "with or together"

        2.   "Mission" = from the Latin word *missio* meaning "a sending away"

B.   Greek Words Denoting Commit or Commission

        1.   Paradidomi = to give over, in the sense of delivery or entrusting something
                to a person (Luke 16:11; I Timothy 1:11)

        2.   Paratithemi = to entrust, commit to one's charge, something to guard (Luke
                12:48; I Timothy 1:18; II Timothy 2:2; I Peter 4:19)

        3.   Parakatatheke = a putting into someone a deposit (II Timothy 1:12; I
                Timothy 6:20)

        4.   Epitrope = a turning over of a specific responsibility to another, so a
                committal of full powers, a commission (Acts 26:12; Acts 26:16,19; Acts
                9:15; Acts 13:2)

C.   Commissioned for Ministry
        1.   The specific task or purpose in which a person is apparently destined in life,
                a calling, a destiny, a mission.
        2.   A being sent out with special authority to perform special duties, an
                authorization to perform certain duties or tasks or to take on certain powers.
        3.   To put a ship into commission, to send a vessel out on a service after it has
                been laid up, to equip and man a vessel for service, hoist the flag, complete
                readiness for service.

IV.   COMMON CHARACTERISTICS OF LEADERS WITH IDENTIFIED MISSION

Oswald Sanders: "Any ambition which centers around and terminates upon oneself is unworthy while an ambition which has the mission of God as its center is not only legitimate but positively praiseworthy."

A.   Commissioned leaders decide to pay any price necessary to advance toward the mission   (I Corinthians 9:24-26; Ecclesiastes 5:3)

B.   Commissioned leaders maintain their focus on the mark in spite of incredible conflicts (Philippians 3:13-14)

C.   Commissioned leaders reach out and seize their mission by force if necessary (Proverbs 24:3)

D.   Commissioned leaders complete successfully their God-ordained mission (II Tim 4:7-11)

E.   Commissioned leaders are characterized by positive biblical attitudes

1.   The Winner's Attitude

2.   The Champion's Attitude

3.   The Conqueror's Attitude

4.   The Overcomer's Attitude

> Do not pray for easy lives.
> Pray to be stronger men.
> Do not pray for tasks equal to your power.
> Pray for power equal to your tasks.

V. MISSION MINDED LEADERS AVOID WRONG THINKING

A. Victim Mode of Thinking

B. Sustainer Mode of Thinking

C. Dreamer Mode of Thinking

D. Controller Mode of Thinking

E. Adventurous Mode of Thinking

F. Positive Mode of Thinking

G. Rut Mode of Thinking

H. Losers Mode of Thinking

VI. MISSION MINDED LEADERS FACE CHANGE SUCCESSFULLY

A. Facing the Uncertainty of Change

B. Facing the Decisions of Change

1. Decide to be flexible at all costs

2. Decide to be advancing all the time

3. Devise a strategy to advance to the leading edge of your calling

4. Decide to be a problem solver in pursuit of God's best

5. Decide to be extraordinarily persistent

6. Decide to be a risk taker

VII. MISSION MINDED LEADERS RISE TO THE CHALLENGE

A. David – A Leader Who Rises to the Challenge

1. Responds to the challenge, not the problem (I Samuel 17:23-27)

2. Does not allow himself to be shaped by circumstances, opinions or criticisms of others (I Samuel 17:28-33)

3. Lives by what God's Word says, not by what he sees, hears or imagines to be true   (I Samuel 17:29)

4. Responds with courage to seemingly impossible challenge (I Samuel 17:31-37,48)

B. Encouragement for Leaders Who Rise to the Challenge
1. Isaiah 41:8-9 I have not rejected you but have chosen you.
2. Isaiah 41:10 Fear not, I am with you. Be not dismayed.
3. Isaiah 41:10 I am your God.
4. Isaiah 41:10 I will strengthen you.
5. Isaiah 41:10 I will uphold you with my victorious right hand.
6. Isaiah 41:11-12 I will destroy all your enemies.
7. Isaiah 41:15 I will make you a sharp threshing instrument.

VIII. MISSION MINDED LEADERS ENJOY THE DISCOVERY OF MISSION

A. Discovering your mission will give purpose, meaning and challenge to your life.

B. Discovering your mission will bring a realization of self-worth to your life.

C. Discovering your mission will turn routine tasks into enjoyable experiences.

D. Discovering your mission will allow you to use all your resources to their greatest efficiency.

E. Discovering your mission will cause new areas of interest to begin to surface in your life.

F. Discovering your mission will cause you to devote all your energy to a definite goal.

G. Discovering your mission will strengthen the many-membered Body of Christ both locally and abroad.

H. Discovering your mission will motivate you to be a faithful steward of what God has placed in your life.

Cultivating a Vision
for God's Eternal Purpose

INTRODUCTION

After the visionary leader has successfully cultivated a personal vision and identified a personal mission, it is necessary to cultivate a clear understanding of God's ultimate purposes. The purpose of God thus becomes a guiding force to all vision accomplishment. Without this, a visionary leader may use his energies toward great ideas but not necessarily a purpose-driven God idea. Not all vision, even good vision with noble causes, are extending the biblically stated purpose of God. This understanding will cause a leader to be very careful, very focused and to spend more time in serious prayer before undertaking vision of any kind.

> Vision is that which a leader and a congregation perceives by the Holy Spirit as pertaining to God's purpose for them, thereby creating spiritual momentum, resulting in spiritual advancement and maintained through spiritual warfare.

I.   **THE POSSIBILITY OF A FAULTY VISION**
      (Jeremiah 14:14; 23:16; 27:9; 23:25-27)

      A.   Vision without biblical ingredients

      B.   Vision with human origination, empowered by human spirits.

      C.   Vision that overly accommodates culture.

      D.   Vision with temporal elements.

II. THE POWER OF FOCUS
(Philippians 3:13-14)

    A.   The Focus Principle

        1.   Focus on Maintaining Biblical Presupposition

        2.   Focus on a Biblical Product

        3.   Focus on Following Biblical Principles

> Leadership must articulate a mission and a set of values that capture the loyalty of the people and provide a sense of direction.

    B.   The Lens That Helps Us to Focus

        1.   The Lens of Scripture

        2.   The Lens of History

        3.   The Lens of Prophecy

        4.   The Lens of the Holy Spirit

III. THE POWER OF UNDERSTANDING GOD'S PURPOSE
(Ephesians 3:8-21; Colossians 1:24-29)

    A.   Understanding the eternal purpose of God is foundational to our life vision, our life philosophy and our level of commitment to the house of God.

    B.   Becoming a Purpose-Driven Leader

        1.   Not driven by comparison or competition

        2.   Not driven by what you see other ministries accomplish

3.   Not driven by your own gifting, desires, dreams

4.   Not driven by successful church visions

5.   Not driven by the winds of other's opinions

      a.   Purposefulness is the clear and dominant sense of what one is seeking to accomplish

      b.   Purposefulness provides a driving force, a compelling sense of urgency that generates and marshals energy.

6.   Not a leader who reverses the means and the ends

      a.   Ends

      b.   Means

IV.   UNDERSTANDING THE BASIC PURPOSE OF GOD – FIRST
(Genesis 1:26-28; Mt 16:16-18; Isaiah 46:10-11; 14:21-27; Jeremiah 4:28; Job 42:2; Ecclesiastes 3:1,7; Ephesians 1:10-11; Isaiah 48:11; Proverbs 19:21)

A.   The Evolution of God's Purpose

    1.   The Purpose of God Revealed in the Covenants (Genesis 1:26-28)
        a.   Relationship
        b.   Character
        c.   Warfare
        d.   Global Glory

    2.   The Eight Basic Covenants
        a.   Edenic Covenant
        b.   Adamic Covenant
        c.   Noahic Covenant
        d.   Abrahamic Covenant
        e.   Mosaic Covenant
        f.   Palestinian Covenant
        g.   Davidic Covenant
        h.   New Covenant

B.   The Execution of God's Purpose

    1.   The cross is the source of mission and the message of mission.

2. The cross is the hermeneutical filter through which all thought must flow.

3. The cross is the key to interpreting the covenants and the prophets.

4. The cross is the dividing point of the Old and New Covenants.

C. The Enunciation of God's Purpose

1. The Extension of God's Kingdom
   (Matthew 4:17-23; Acts 20:25; 28:23-31; Hebrews 12:28; Revelation 11:15)

2. The Establishing of Christ's Church
   (Ephesians 5:25-32)

3. The Expectancy of Christ's Return
   (John 14:3; I Thessalonians 4:16; I John 2:28)

V. COVENANTAL THEOLOGY VS DISPENSATIONAL THEOLOGY
◄ *One's theological system determines one's vision for the church* ➤

A. Establishing Vision Upon Sound Theology

1. Understand covenantal theology and the accusation of replacement theology

2. Understand traditional dispensationalism

3. Understand natural Israel's place in God's plan (not anti-Semitic)

4. Understand how basic theology impacts one's vision for the church

B. Identifying the Different Schools of Theology

1. Replacement theology

2. Dominion theology

3. Reconstructionist theology

4. Restoration theology

5. Dispensational theology

6. Jewish theology

C.   Covenantal Theology Defined
     Covenantal Theology is a theological system which views God's plan as a single
     Divine purpose (essentially soteriological), namely the restoration of man to God
     through the redemption of Christ. This plan is administered on the basis of covenant
     in redemptive history in a covenanted people, Israel. National Israel is later cast
     away because of unbelief, and the church becomes the covenanted community,
     Spiritual Israel.

D.   Dispensational Theology Defined
     Dispensational theology is a theological system which views God's plan as various
     different administrations in redemptive history (called dispensations) in which each
     dispensation has a separate Divine purpose peculiar to it. This plan is seen as an
     interrupted progression in which God has two people with perpetually differing
     prophetic plans: the earthly seed, national Israel, and the heavenly seed, the church.

     1.   *Historic Dispensationalism*: views the church in God's prophetic program
          as awaiting the second coming of Christ. The church is seen to have no
          particular destiny on earth in God's prophetic plan.

     2.   *Neo-Dispensationalism*: States there is one new covenant with a two-fold
          application: one primarily for national Israel in the future and secondarily
          one to the church now. This theory says that the Christian has all the
          blessings of the new covenant but cannot explain how Christians receive
          these blessings apart from any real relationship to the New Covenant.

E.   Contrast of Ultimate Results of the Two Theologies

Covenantal Theology	**Dispensational Theology**
Sees the church as being restored to the truth of power of God and becoming a glorious, victorious church in the last days.	Sees the church as having no particular destiny on earth in God's prophetic plan.
Sees God's plan as progressive with divine continuity through the ages.	Denies any unity of God's plan or God's people throughout the ages and denies a continuity of God's program.
Believes the New Testament church is based on the New Covenant.	Believes that the New Covenant is with Israel and the church has no direct relationship to the New Covenant.
Espouses a balance between the church as the instrument of God and the kingdom as the purpose of God.	Believes the church has no real relationship to God's purpose.
Believes that end-time prophecies are directly fulfilled in and by the church.	Denies any direct fulfillment of end-time prophecies in and by the church.

VI.   THE CHURCH IS GOD'S FUTURE
(Ephesians 5:25-31)

A.   Church is God's eternal purpose
(Ephesians 3:10-11; Isaiah 14:7; 55:8-11; 48:11)

B.   Church is the great mystery of God
(Ephesians 3:3-4,9; 5:32)

C.   Church is the new ethnic holy nation
(I Corinthians 12:13)

D.   Church is the army of God
(Matthew 16:16-18; II Corinthians 10:4-5)

E.   Church is the body of Christ on earth
(I Corinthians 12; Ephesians 4)

F.   Church is the harvesting tool
(Revelation 14:14-16; Matthew 9:35-37)

G.   Church is the Bride of Christ
(Ephesians 5:25-31; Revelation 19:7-9)

H.   Church is to be triumphant and victorious
(Matthew 16:16-18; Genesis 22:17; 24:60)

A Church Vision Believes:
- The church precedes, transcends and succeeds Israel.
- The church is the ultimate and final instrument of God that will reveal God's wisdom and glory to this world.
- The church will become glorious and triumphant prior to the coming of Christ.
- The church will reap a harvest of souls from every nation, tribe, kindred and people prior to Christ's second coming.

Cultivating a Vision Within Today's Culture

INTRODUCTION

Biblical vision and the 21st century modern day culture are destined to clash in every way possible. The shifts that have taken place in today's value system have been mega-shifts. The humanistic, syncretistic philosophy of our American culture has eroded almost all moral value systems. We now face a new culture, a culture separated from God and His word. The challenge of today's leadership is to establish godly vision, teach godly values and confront modern day culture.

The word "culture" comes from the Latin *colore* which means "to till" or "to cultivate." It refers, not only to tilling the soil, but also the mind, the heart and the emotions. In the broadest sense, culture may be defined as "the total pattern of human behavior and its products embodied in thought, speech, action and artifacts and dependent upon man's capacity for learning and transmitting knowledge to succeeding generations through the use of tools, languages and systems of abstract thought. (Robert Webber)

I. VIEWS OF MODERN DAY CULTURE

A. Modern Day Culture in Biblical Context

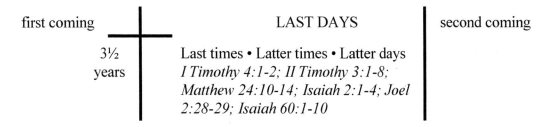

first coming   LAST DAYS   second coming

3½ years

Last times • Latter times • Latter days
I Timothy 4:1-2; II Timothy 3:1-8;
Matthew 24:10-14; Isaiah 2:1-4; Joel
2:28-29; Isaiah 60:1-10

1. Last Day's Culture: Aids, abortion, infanticide, divorce in one out of two marriages, increase in unmarried mothers, single parent homes, child negligence, homosexual marriages, information overload, unreal reality, transnational data flow, drug crisis, air pollution, ozone layer depletion, vanishing species fear, spreading deserts, water shortages, poverty, unemployment, homelessness, crime, loss of cultures, fragile economies, disorder in financial markets, rise of new age, cultism, humanism, society rejecting God and His word.

2. Last Day's Deception (Matthew 24:4-5; I Timothy 4:1-2; I Timothy 4:2)

B. Modern Day Culture and Man's View of the Future
    (Isaiah 41:23; Matthew 16:2-4; Acts 16:16)
    1. The booming global economy
    2. A renaissance in the arts
    3. The emergence of free market socialism
    4. Global lifestyles and cultural nationalism
    5. The privatization of the welfare state

6. The rise of the Pacific Rim
7. The decade of women in leadership
8. The age of biology
9. The religious revival of the new millennium
10. The triumph of the individual

C. Modern Day Culture's Predictions Concerning the New World Culture
1. A larger world. If you are 50 years old, the world has doubled in your lifetime.
2. A developing world. By 2000 80% of the population will be in developing countries and 60% will be in Asian countries.
3. An older world. By 2025 there will be one billion people over 60; that is one in seven.
4. A younger world. 60% of the population is now under 24. Half of Latin America is under 18. Mexico City has a population under 14 that is equal to New York City's entire population. There is not a third world city with a median age over 20!
5. An urban world. Mexico City will have 31 million people by the year 2000. By then there will be at least 22 mega cities with populations of more than ten million.
6. A potential conflict world. 50% of our scientific minds are engaged in so-called defense. Many fully expect a nuclear terrorist incident between the nuclear nations by the year 2000.
7. An information era. It will be a world divided, not by the have and the have not's, but by the know and the know not's. We can now send the Encyclopedia Britannica across the Atlantic six times a minute. If the auto industry would keep up with the computer information advance, a Rolls Royce would get three million miles to the gallon, would cost less than three dollars and you could put six on the head of a pin.
8. A different world in religion. Islam is growing 16% a year; Hinduism 12%; Buddhism 10%; Christianity 9%. There are now more Muslims than Baptists in Britain. By the year 2000 the number of missionaries from Latin America and Asia may exceed those from North America. North America and Europe will be seen increasingly as spiritually bankrupt for all our success and our technology and hedonism.

II. SHIFTS IN CULTURE

A. Shift in World Culture
1. Shift in Science: from modern science to modern modern science.
2. Shift in Philosophy: from optimism to pessimism and existentialism.
3. Shift in Theology: from biblical absolutes to higher criticism.
4. Shift in Morality: from rules of morality to situation ethics, from amoral to immoral society.
5. Shift from Absolutes to Relativism
6. Shift from Monotheism to Polytheism

B. Shifts in Lifestyle Culture
   1. Cocooning
   2. Decency Decade
   3. Cashing Out
   4. "Now" Decade
   5. Fantasy Adventure
   6. Religious Decade
   7. Humanism and Syncretism

C. Shifts in Moral Culture
   (Acts 2:40; Phil 2:5; Mt 24:12; Acts 1:25; Rom 1:16-32)
   1. No God-given moral laws
   2. No objective moral laws
   3. No timeless moral laws
   4. No laws against laws
   5. No restraints to pleasures
   6. No restrictions to pleasures
   7. No restrictions to individual choices
   8. No absolutes or principles to live by

D. Shifts in Church Culture
   1. From biblical preaching to innovative communication
   2. From absolutes to pragmatism
   3. From theology to methodology
   4. From sanctification to worldliness
   5. From evangelism to marketing
   6. From spiritual worship to visitor sensitive programs

E. Shifts in the Philosophy of Culture

   1. Insights Into Our Culture
      a. Chuck Colson: "A common thread runs through these images – the notion that life somehow gives us the right to have every whim and desire satisfied. Driven in the pursuit of pleasure, society has become miserable. The society we live in has developed a Disney philosophy. Disney is but a picture of the world at large who tend to exhaust themselves on the mistaken notion that multiplying pleasures produces happiness. 20th century wrath of God has been dismissed as the product of Puritan prudence. Right and wrong are no longer moral absolutes to live by but psychological hang-ups to be healed! It strikes me that the prevalent characteristic of our culture today is rampant narcissism, materialism and hedonism. Our culture passes itself off as Christian with 50 million Americans, according to George Gallup, claiming to be born-again. But, it is dominated almost entirely by relativism. The 'do your own thing' mindset has liberated us from the absolute structure of faith and belief and sent us adrift in a sea of nothingness."

b. Frederick More Vinson: "Nothing is more certain in modern society than the principle that there are no absolutes; all is relative; all is experience. The only absolute allowed is the absolute insistence that there is no absolute."

c. Francis Shaeffer: "The American people adopted two impoverished values: personal peace and personal affluence."
   - Personal peace: Just to be let alone, not to be troubled by the trouble of other people, whether across the world or across the street. To live one's life with minimal possibilities of being personally disturbed, wanting to have my personal life pattern undisturbed in my lifetime regardless of what the results will be in the lifetime of my children or grandchildren.
   - Personal affluence: An overwhelming and ever-increasing prosperity; a life made up of things, things and more things. A success judged by an ever higher level of material abundance.

2. Modern Day Philosophies

   a. *The Legalistic Philosophy*: With this approach, one enters into every decision-making situation encumbered with a whole apparatus of prefabricated rules and regulations. Its principles, codified in rules, are not merely guidelines or maxims to illuminate the situation; they are directives to be followed. Solutions are in the rule book – the Bible.

   b. *The Antinomian Philosophy* (Against Law): This is the approach with which one enters into the decision-making situation armed with no principles or maxims whatsoever, to say nothing of rules. In every "existential moment" or "unique" situation, it declares one must rely upon the situation of itself, there and then, to provide its ethical solution.

   c. *The Existentialist Philosophy*: A complicated, and often hard to define, philosophical perspective. The word "existentialist" applies to many artists, composers, poets and playwrights as well as to philosophers, theologians and biblical scholars. If there is a single thread which runs through the ideas of all those who are called existentialists, it would be the following:

   - A voice of protest aimed at all forces at work which institutionalize and dehumanize mankind.
   - The emphasis upon the will and the act of man, as opposed to his rational capacity and ability to formulate truth.
   - Focus on the inner-consciousness and subjectivity, rather than fixed absolutes known by reason (note: pure reason leads to paradox).
   - Emphasis upon the "human condition", expressing man's plight in terms of the feeling of dread, anxiety, forlornness, death and the possibility of non-existence (note: all existentialism amplifies man's dark side and is rooted in deep pessimism).

- "Man is condemned to freedom (Sartre)." Although man has no ultimate satisfaction in finding truth by reason, he must make choices. Choice leads to meaning and value!

d. *The Situationist Philosophy*: The situationist enters every decision-making situation fully armed with the ethical maxims of his community and its heritage and he tries to treat them with respect as illuminators of his problems. Just the same, he is prepared in any situation to compromise them and sets them aside in the situation if love seems better served by doing so. Circumstances alter rules and principles.

e. *The Pragmatist Philosophy*: Pragmatism to the plain-spoken is a practical or success posture. Whatever brings satisfaction and whatever works is right and good. This idiom expresses the genius and philosophy of style or life of American culture and of the techno-scientific era. Pragmatism says, "To be correct or right a thing, a thought or an action must work. The end justifies the means."

f. *The Relativistic Philosophy*: The shift away from the rules of rationality to acceptance of unconscious and motivational dynamics as the foundation of human behavior; a shift, which is clearly visible in any situation ethic, from a hierarchy of values, ranged in some supposedly given and permanent order of bad or better, to a fluid spectrum of values. What is one man's meat is another man's poison in a kind of "absolute relativism."

g. *The Humanistic Philosophy*: Secular humanism is a religion that dethrones God as the center of life and enshrines man instead. The aim of secular humanism is to replace theism with humanism. The tenets of humanism are atheism, evolution, amorality, autonomous man and a socialist, one world view. Regarding amorality, the *Humanist Manifesto* says, "In the area of sexuality we believe that intolerant attitudes are often cultivated by orthodox religions which unduly repress sexual conduct. The right to birth control, abortion and divorce should be recognized. Neither do we wish to prohibit sexual behavior between consenting adults."

h. *Ethical Egoism*: The philosophy that posits: nothing is more valuable than the individual self; or the self is the only thing valuable. One's ethic, therefore, is derived from the "virtue of selfishness." Those acts, decision and relationships which directly contribute to oneself are called "good" and those which bear no contribution to the self are deemed "bad" or worthless. Ethical behavior thus followed from the deliberate and calculated maxim: "What's in it for me?"

i. ***Psychological Egoism*** (a la Bishop J. Butler): Distinct from yet related to ethical egoism, psychological egoism argues that all people do act out of concern for self and therefore all people are selfish to a certain extent. Butler argued that the human consciousness is divided over doing good for others and benefiting self. Psychological egoism is passive rather than active in the sense that it says people are basically selfish, rather than saying that people ought to be selfish. Psychological egoism posits that people can act out of altruistic and egoistic motives at the same time (e.g. someone who feeds the poor, exhibiting compassion, but subconsciously expects a reward (heaven, eternal life).

III. KINGDOM CULTURE AND WORLD CULTURE TENSION

A. A Culture Within A Culture

B. The Continual Tension
(II Peter 2:7-19; II Corinthians 11:2; John 17:11-15; I John 2:15; Romans 12:2)

C. World Culture Tensions

1. Moral tensions

2. Lifestyle tensions

3. Value tensions

4. Media tensions

5. Music

> "Nothing is more singular about this generation than its addiction to music. This is the age of music and the states of soul that accompany it. Today a very large population, the portion of young people between ages of 10 and 25, live for music. It is their passion. Nothing else excites them as it does. They cannot take seriously anything alien to music. Nothing surrounding them — school, family, church — has anything to do with their musical world. At best, that ordinary life is neutral, but mostly it is an impediment, drained of vital content, even a thing to be rebelled against." (Allan Bloom, Closing of the American Mind, pg 68)
>
> "The world view of modern man shapes modern music. Man is isolated and helpless in the grip of forces he does not understand; he has fallen prey to inner conflict, tension, anxiety and fear." (Francis Shaeffer)

C.   The Charismatic Movement Dilemma
(I Timothy 3:15)

    1.   1950 – 1990
       a. Gifts displayed
       b. Charismatic leaders
       c. Mega churches

    2.   1990's – 2000
       a. Immorality and adultery among church leadership
       b. Lesbians in priesthood and ordination of homosexuals
       c. Lack of fear of God
       d. Holiness seen as legalism

D.   The Church of Today and Its Struggles Within Complex Culture

    1.   Denial

    2.   Mixed Message

    3.   Remnant Withdrawal Syndrome

    4.   Fad Addiction

    5.   Leaping and Creeping

IV.   ELEMENTS THAT SHAPE CULTURE

A.   The Three Main Forces

    1.   The Philosophic Element

    2.   The Scientific Element

    3.   The Religious Element

B.   Freeway of the Flow of Culture

    1.   The Invisible Aspect of Culture

    2.   The Visible Aspect of Culture

C.	Cultivating a World View

1.	The grid through which he sees the world

2.	The basic way we look at life

3.	The perception of what is truth

4.	The basis for our values and therefore our decisions

D.	Methods of Facing Culture

1.	Academia

2.	Tradition

3.	Experiential

4.	Biblical

E.	Vision to Penetrate Today's Culture

1.	To penetrate our culture with the kingdom of God and to resist culturized Christianity as a disease that neutralizes the true power of the gospel.

2.	To recruit people from the world to become part of Christ's community and movement.

3.	To equip and mobilize those people to live and function both in the local church and in their particular world environment.

The Scope of Vision Definition

I. **THE LINGUISTIC DEFINITION**

    A.   Hebrew: To gaze at, mentally perceive, to contemplate with pleasure the things of the future.

    B.   Dictionary: The act or power of sensing with the eyes, power of anticipation and expectation.

    C.   Greek: (skopos) A mark on which to fix the eyes, as a runner who is looking toward the goal line (Philippians 3:13-14).

II. **CONCEPTUAL DEFINITION**

    A.   Vision is that which a congregation perceives by the Holy Spirit as pertaining to God's purpose for them, thereby creating spiritual momentum resulting in spiritual advancement and maintained through spiritual warfare.

    B.   Vision is having a view from above.

    C.   Vision is the ability of seeing into the future, having foresight into something which is attainable to a person or a group.

    D.   Vision is the product of God working in us. God creates the vision, we receive it, and the vision becomes a rallying point, a goal toward which we move as His chosen people.

    E.   Vision is the result of the church willing to rise to the full challenge of commitment as revealed in the scriptures.

    F.   Vision is an inspired look at reality.

    G.   Vision is foresight with insight based on hindsight.

    H.   Vision is seeing the invisible and making it visible.

    I.   Vision is an informed bridge from the present to the future.

    J.   Vision is a clear mental image of a preferable future imparted by God through His chosen servants and is based upon an accurate understanding of God, self and circumstances (Barna).

III. NECESSARY INGREDIENTS TO HEALTHY BIBLICAL VISION

A. Healthy Biblical Vision Must Be Biblically Accurate
(I Corinthians 3:8-12)

B. Healthy Biblical Vision Must Be Spiritually Grasped
(I Corinth 1:10-16; Ephesians 1:18; Matthew 9:29-30; Luke 24:16,31; Gen 21:19)

C. Healthy Biblical Vision Must Be Balanced

D. Healthy Biblical Vision Must Be Progressive
(Genesis 3:15; 22:17; 24:60)

IV. THE APOSTLE PAUL'S VISION FOR THE CHURCH
(Ephesians 5:26-33)

A. That He might sanctify her and cleanse her by the washing of water by the Word
(Ephesians 5:26-28)

B. That He might present her
(Ephesians 5:26-29)

C. That He might have a glorious church
(Ephesians 3:10)

D. That He might have a church without spot
(II Peter 2:13-14; Jude 1:12,23)

E. That He might have a church not having wrinkle
(Ephesians 5:29-31)

F. That He might have a holy church
(II Corinthians 11:1-3; I Peter 2:9)

G. That He might have a church without blemish
(Ephesians 1:4; Colossians 1:22; Hebrews 9:14; Jude 1:24; Revelation 14:5)

The Four Levels of Vision

INTRODUCTION

As a leader develops a biblical vision, all levels of vision must be comprehended. A "working from the part to the whole and the whole to the part" principle must be applied. Vision must work from the universal or world sphere to the local and regional sphere. The four levels of vision are world, national, regional and local. The local vision will be our emphasis as we develop a full and biblical vision.

I. FOUR LEVELS OF BIBLICAL VISION

    A.   Vision Of God's Plan On A Universal Level
            (Mark 11:17; Joel 2:28; Daniel 2:7; Matthew 16:18-20)

    B.   Vision of God's Plan on a National Level
            (Daniel 3:29; Revelation 5:9; 14:6; Isaiah 2:1-4; Psalm 72:11)

    C.   Vision of God's Plan on a Regional Level
            (Acts 13:49; 14:6, 27; 17:16; 18:10; Isaiah 54:3; Matthew 4:16; II Corinthians 10:6)

    D.   Vision of God's Plan on a Local Church Level
            (Revelation 1:20; Matthew 16:16-18; 18:16-20; Philippians 1:1-3)

II. THE VISION FOR THE LOCAL CHURCH EXPANDED

    A.   The Gate Church – A Local Church Model
            (Genesis 28:10-22)

        1.   The spiritual atmosphere of the Gate-church
                (Genesis 28:12; II Chronicles 31:2)

        2.   The Gate-Church prayer intercession ladder
                (Isaiah 56:7; Genesis 28:12)

        3.   The Gate-Church implements present prophetic truths
                (Genesis 28:13,15; Isaiah 62:10)

        4.   The Gate Church Grows in Quantity and Quality
                (Genesis 28:13-14)

        5.   The Gate Church Blesses and Builds Families
                (Genesis 28:14)

        6.   The Gate-Church Door of Divine Opportunity
                (Genesis 28:15)

        7.   The Gate Church Has Awesome Worship
                (Genesis 28:16-17; II Chronicles 5:11-14; Isaiah 60:18; Psalm 24:7)

8. The Gate Church Builds with Stones and Pillars
(II Chronicles 2:1-10; Genesis 28:18-19; I Kings 5:17-18; I Peter 2:5)

9. The Gate Church is a Word-Driven Church
(Genesis 28:19)

10. The Gate Church Is a Giving Church
(Genesis 28:20-22; Is 60:11)

11. The Gate Church Opens the Gate of Healing and Miracles
(John 1:50-51)

B. Our vision of a local church from the book of Acts
1. A powerful church, Acts 1:8
2. A praying church, Acts 1:14
3. A unified church, Acts 1:14; 2:1
4. A Spirit-filled church, Acts 2:1; 4:38
5. A word church, Acts 2:42
6. A reverent church, Acts 2:43
7. A sharing church, Acts 2:44-45
8. A gathering together church, Acts 2:46
9. A supernatural church, Acts 2:44-45
10. A fellowshipping church, Acts 2:46
11. A happy church, Acts 2:46
12. A worshipping church, Acts 2:46; 15:15-17
13. A likeable church, Acts 2:47-48
14. A witnessing church, Acts 1:8
15. A growing-expanding church, Acts 2:42-48
16. A missionary sending church, Acts 13:1-6; 15:36
17. A leadership training church, Acts 4,11,13,15
18. A society penetrating church, Acts 17:6
19. A church with elders and deacons, Acts 6:1-7; 14:23; 16:1-10; 16:4
20. A church with the gifts of the Holy Spirit, I Cor 12,14

C. Vision of a Local Church from the Church at Antioch[1]
1. A biblically founded church: preaches Christ as the one and only foundation for repentance and faith unto salvation (Acts 8:5; Acts 8:12; Acts 9:20; 1 Cor 3:9-16)
2. A church having a senior leader: there must be a senior leader, a presiding elder to oversee the affairs of the church, giving direction to the church under Christ's headship. This leading elder is the "messenger" (Grk *angelos*, Rev 1-3) of the church, as in the local churches of Asia.
3. A church having plurality of ministries: No one man can bear the whole burden of a larger church. Plurality of ministry team is necessary for checks and balances in team ministry.

---

[1] Kevin Conner

4. A church that taught and trained disciples: All believers are called to be disciples and need to be discipled, trained, instructed in the ways of the Lord. A disciple is a true Christian, a follower of Christ and lives as a Christian should live. (Acts 11:26; Matt 28:19; Acts 14:21)

5. A church having a balance of ministries. Both inspirational (prophets) and instructional (teachers) are needed to maintain balance in the church. Plurality, diversity, variety yet unity of word and spirit. (Acts 13:1)

6. A church that ministered to the Lord: A worshipping church, to minister to the Lord, serve Him, wait on Him and be in right relationship with Him first of all. All else springs out of this relationship with Christ. (Acts 13:2; 1 Sam 3:1; 2 Chr 29:11)

7. A church that prayed and fasted: An Antioch church is a praying church. Fasting should be experienced at times both individually and corporately as the Lord directs. Fasting subdues the flesh and intensifies our seeking the Lord. Helps rid the church of unbelief, makes one spiritually alert, sensitive to the mind of the Spirit. (Acts 13:2-3; Mark 2:18-20)

8. A church that allowed the Holy Spirit to speak: Desires to be open and sensitive to what the Spirit would say and have an ear to hear and obey what He says through the Word, the ministries and the gifts of the members. (Acts 13:2; Acts 8:29)

9. A church that recognized and received the prophetic word: Recognizes and receives the prophetic word that comes over it through various prophetic ministries and wars a good warfare by the prophetic word. (I Timothy 1:18-19)

10. A church that believed and received the laying on of hands: Believes in the laying on of hands in the various areas mentioned in scripture: blessing, healing, baptism of the Spirit, confirmation, ordination, etc. (Acts 13:3; Hebrews 6:1-2; I Timothy 5:22)

11. A church that received the revelation of the Tabernacle of David: The revelation of salvation through grace and faith apart from animal sacrifices and ceremonies of the law; a revelation of the Davidic order of worship, song and praise. It is a revelation of access within the veil and that worship which is in spirit and in truth. (Acts 15:16-17)

12. A church that became a great evangelistic/missionary church: From Antioch, a number of other churches were planted.

III. TEN HIGHLIGHTS OF VISION
(Sample from City Bible Church)

A. *A world vision church*. There are 239 nations and 350 large world-cities that need apostolic churches. We need to raise up an apostolic leader and apostolic church for every city. We need at least 10,000 new church plants with 2,000 New Testament elders and 10,000 apostolic worship leaders. We need a world faith for a world vision! We by ourselves can't do this, but we can partner with the Body of Christ, mark our cities and do our share.

B. *An apostolic church in character and attitude.* This describes a church with proven apostolic doctrine; a believing, receiving and functioning of the five-fold ministry and New Testament eldership with an emphasis on spiritual fathers and spiritual sons and daughters; an Acts 11, Antioch church vision. "Apostolic is from the root meaning of the Greek word *apostolos* which means one who is sent with a commission. Apostolic churches, by nature, give a high priority to reaching out effectively to the unchurched."

George Hunter: "I delineate the distinctiveness of 'apostolic congregations' along lines like these: (1) Their main business, often the obsession, is to reach and disciple lost people; (2) Like the ancient apostles and the churches they planted, they study, profile, and target a distinct, largely-undiscipled population, not merely lost individuals; (3) To reach that population, they adapt their music, language, liturgy, leadership style, etc., to fit the culture of the target population; (4) They have a distinct (apostolic) vision of what people, as disciples, can become; and (5) They are driven to experience, and they do experience, substantial conversion growth from the world." (C. Peter Wagner. Churchquake!)

George G. Hunter III of Asbury Theological Seminary gives ten characteristics of apostolic congregations: strong biblical content; earnest in prayer; compassion for the lost; obedience to the Great Commission; vision for what people can become; cultural adaptation to the target population; small groups; strong lay ministries; every member and every seeker receives regular pastoral care—from a layperson; many ministries to the unchurched.

According to Elmer Towns of Liberty University, the following are characteristics of new apostolic churches: large size; family feeling, but not exclusive; cross socioeconomic classes; led by 'charismatic' pastor-leaders; congregation both independent and interdependent; reflect New Testament theological bias; passion for outpouring of God's Spirit; bonded by methodology, not theology. C. Peter Wagner describes them as follows: new name; new authority structure; new leadership training; new ministry focus; new worship style; new prayer forms; new financing; new outreach; new power priorities.

C. *A prayer-intercession focused church.* More prayer is better than less prayer. We must invest money, time, staff and energy to raising a praying church. Prayer should be moved back into the sanctuary to be part of the main services as the main thing. Intercessory prayer needs to be practiced by all levels within the church with a prayer pastor, a prayer center opened 24 hours a day, days of prayer, prayer cards, and prayer leaders. Prayer must permeate every aspect of the praying church. Adding a prayer elder or prayer pastor has been a fruitful decision for us. Someone must help carry the burden and continually pastor specialized intercessors, implement prayer ideas, and meet with prayer leaders in every group. We just implemented a fifteen minute Partners in Prayer strategy. This is a plan that calls the whole church to pray for the senior pastor, his wife and family for fifteen minutes a day. The card has specific requests from the pastor. Depending on how many people in your church do this, the amount of prayer will be in the hundreds of hours daily, weekly and monthly. This is another way to encourage target prayer.

D.	*A worshipping church with freedom and creativity.* This will not happen automatically. There must be much prayer and teaching, mentoring, changes made continually. We added a Thursday night School of David, which stands for **D**avidic worship, **A**rts, **V**oice, **I**nstruments and **D**rama. These five parts of our worship department meet on Thursdays for half an hour of prayer-intercession, half an hour of teaching and then practical preparation from 8:00 – 9:30 p.m. This has allowed us to put vision, biblical principles, right thinking, commitment, purity, music unity and purpose deep into the whole department. I personally took leadership of the prayer and teaching for almost two years and now still do it the first Thursday of each month. Our vision is to upgrade our worship and our worship department. We need pastoral leadership in the worship ministry to disciple and mentor our musicians. We need new songs need to be written that reflect the DNA of the church.

E.	*A "change your life" deliverance/counseling church.* People have more complex mental, spiritual, emotional and flesh problems than in the past. People need more understanding of who they are in Christ, what the biblical standards are for them to achieve, how to break patterns of sin habit and about demonic activity. Deliverance will become a ministry within many local churches. There will be many different flavors, but the goal will be the same: to set people free. Truth encounters must be coupled with power encounters. We are building into our theology, our practice and our budget room for ministering more deeply and more broadly to all people for all problems.

F.	*A build and heal your family church.* More demands on the family calls for more resources and ministry from the churches. 21st century families will be, and are, hungry for biblical teaching on the biblical family, on the role of the father, mother and children, on blended family tensions, on authority issues, and on moral complexity. The church must specifically strategize its ministry to all aspects of the family with a family pastor, family resource center, family counseling, family teacher, married small groups, retreats, single parents groups. All of these can be a functional part of the 21st century church. Do not neglect this mighty ministry of today's church. Families will make their choices based on the church's ability to minister to these needs. You can do this!

G.	*An equip every believer church.* We use the word equip quite often. We believe in equipping. We want all leaders to be equipped, and of course, every believer needs to be equipped as well. We had to take a long, hard look at our teaching ministry and make needed changes to truly fulfill the vision of equipping consistently. We developed our School of Equipping, which takes place on the first and third Sunday evenings of each month (our cells meet on the 2nd and 4th Sundays). The School of Equipping is a curriculum built around eight major areas: Church Life, Family Life, Spiritual Growth, Bible Truths, Youth Issues, Prayer-Intercession, Harvest Ministries and Intercultural Ministries.

H.   *A city-reaching, pastor-networking, harvesting church.* Our call is not for our church only but to our city and region. To be a metro city-reaching church we must work together with the whole church to take the whole metro-area. It is overwhelming unless we take one step at a time. I believe healthy churches will be soul-winning churches, churches that see every neighborhood as a place to evangelize. The spiritual water level of our metro city is directly connected to the spiritual water level of our metro city churches. I see our goal as helping cause that spiritual water level to rise in every church. If the pastoral ministry team is spiritually healthy, there is just cause to believe the church will also be healthy. Three or four pastors began gathering in my office for prayer, relationship, discussions and troubleshooting. Over the past two years that group of three or four has grown to 37 committed pastors who have, over the course of time, developed meaningful relationships, written a pastors' covenant, meet the first Sunday of the year for a metro-city communion service and have protected our region from incoming questionable ministries by joining together to ask questions and expect answers. This works well when it is forty pastors of the same metro city asking questions instead of just one pastor. It really is practical and a real way to affect our cities. It is not fast; it is not magical; it is not easy, but the fruit is tangible and long-lasting.

I.   *An all people, all races together church.* This has been one of the most fulfilling and exciting ministries of our church. We have always desired to reach the nations of the world but hadn't really reached the nations at our door. I believe there is an abundance of harvest among the ethnic groups of our cities. They are open to the true gospel, a gospel clothed in love and compassion, a gospel that reaches out to them for fellowship, meals together, making it culturally easy for them to participate.

J.   *A pastor every person with intentional care church.* As the church grows because of prayer, evangelism and healthy vision, the need for pastoring and discipling every person becomes increasingly important. We are focusing our energies into this area of our church with strategy and structure.

The Vision Building Leader

INTRODUCTION

The making of vision has its roots in the making of the leader himself or herself. As the leader matures in spirit and biblical knowledge, the vision itself also matures and deepens. The first foundation stone for the leader who will build a great vision is to understand the non-negotiables of vision. These non-negotiables will always guide the vision builder in the right direction without taking unnecessary detours.

> *A visionary with a Joseph integrity, anointed with an Elijah spirit, that builds God's vision with Pauline theology and a Christ-like dedication.*

I. **THE NON-NEGOTIABLES OF VISION**

    A.   Vision Begins with the Written Word of God
        (Hebrews 1:1-2; Isaiah 28:13)

        1.   The Analyst Approach
            (Exodus 25:9; I Chronicles 28:11-12,19)

        2.   The Revelation Approach
            (Numbers 12:6; Joel 2:28; I Corinthians 2:7-16; Ephesians 1:17)

        3.   The Basic Hermeneutical Approach
            (Luke 24:27; II Timothy 2:15)

    B.   Vision Begins with the Biblically Stated Purpose of God
        (Genesis 1:26-28; Ephesians 3:10-11; 5:27-31)

    C.   Vision Begins Within Its Unique Setting

        1.   The Time

        2.   The Place

        3.   The Culture

II.   VISION AND THE VISION-LEADER

A.   Vision Is Influenced by the Leader's Life
(Nehemiah 2:12; Exodus 24-25)

    1.   Theological Background

    2.   Spiritual Genes

    3.   Mentoring Influences

    4.   Personality

    5.   Educational Journey

    6.   Ministry Exposure

    7.   Integrity Status

    8.   Ministry Experiences

B.   Vision is Imparted to the Leadership Team

    1.   God's vision for a local church is caught by the eldership and leadership team, who by virtue of their submission to God and His ordained leadership and their unique calling, may confirm, clarify, enhance or reject the vision.

    2.   God's vision is further communicated and refined as the leadership team presents a unified voice to the individual members of the local church. The vision is articulated clearly by the senior pastor, confirmed by other leaders, and received by those who have identified themselves with the local assembly.

    3.   The vision should be written out in a clear, brief vision statement identifying the mission of the church.

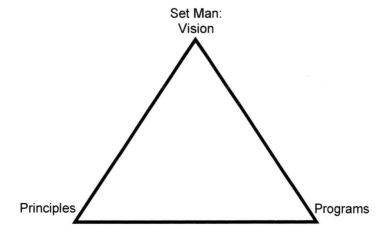

III. LEADERSHIP STYLES THAT INFLUENCE VISION

A. Leadership Styles Spectrum

    1. Autocratic

    2. Participatory

    3. Visionary

    4. Analytical

    5. Motivational

    6. Risk Takers

    7. Transforming Leaders

    8. Prophetic Type

    9. Explorers

    10. Administrator Type Leaders

    11. Trouble Shooters

    12. Traditionalists

    13. Catalysts

    14. Reactor

    15. Creator

B. Leadership Style Discerned

IV. VISION LEADERS COMMON PITFALLS

A. Tendency to become upset when others do not share the same vision or goals

B. Tendency to develop outer callousness due to being a target for criticism.

Twelve Traits of Outstanding Leaders

1. They are note-takers and constant learners.

2. They seek constant improvement.

3. They take pleasure in another's effort.

4. They know the details of their operation.

5. They are visionaries; they have dreams.

6. They listen to subordinates.

7. They meet people outside the office seeking feedback.

8. They give rapt attention to others.

9. They have a passionate hatred of bureaucracy.

10. They pay attention to a few key indicators.

11. They love their product or service.

12. They have a sincere concern for loss in quality.

Celebrate Excellence News, September 1987.

C.   Tendency to use people to accomplish vision at any cost.

D.   Tendency to drive self and neglect personal and family needs

E.   Tendency to neglect routine home responsibilities due to intense interest in the fulfilling of vision

V.   VISION LEADERS COMMON THINGS THAT DULLS THE CUTTING EDGE

A.   Lack of prayer

B.   Fear of being vulnerable

C.   Listening to people rather than God

D.   Listening to a murmurer

E.   Distractions becoming louder than God's word

F.   People pleaser

G.   Lack of prayer and fasting

H.   Lack of feeding in the word

I.   Broken relationships

J.   Fear of being hurt

K.   Fear of rejection

L.   Don't like people who are made at you

M.   Run in overload

N.   Depression

O.   Fear of failure

P.   Lack of proper communication with senior pastor

Q.   Concentrating on doing rather than being

R.   Not sufficient time with God

S.   Ministerial

T.   Doubleminded

U.   Impatience

V.   Holding things in

W.   Cynical and negative

X.   Disappointments

Y.   Lack of confidence

Z.   Preoccupation with Temporal Things

AA.   Not Knowing How to Rest

BB.   Slothfulness/Lack of Vision

The Developing of a Vision Statement

INTRODUCTION

The vision statements are harder work than they probably appear at first glance. How could a few words be that much work? The work of developing a vision statement is part of the process in building a leadership team that owns the vision. It would be quite easy to write down a few great sounding, highly motivating words and feel that you have accomplished the task, but you have not even begun. A vision statement is a reflection of the core values, purpose and mission of your vision. It should be a team effort and team owned.

I.   VISION STATEMENT PROCESS

      A.   Starts with a visionary leader

            1.   Who understands the basic, non-negotiable ingredients.

            2.   Who has articulated the guiding values and principles that govern the implementation of the vision.

            3.   Who has the wisdom, courage, character and anointing to serve the vision.

            4.   Who has the wisdom to align the vision and practice with reality.

      B.   Cultivated with leadership team

            1.   Why is alignment important?

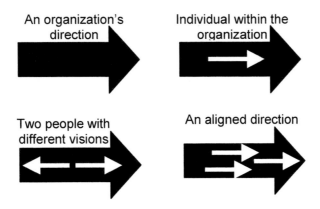

An organization's direction

Individual within the organization

Two people with different visions

An aligned direction

2.   What does effective alignment look like?

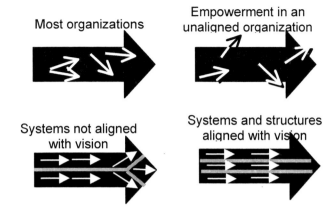

C.   Shared with all levels of congregation

     1.   The ability to teach, feed and nurture the congregation with the vision.

     2.   The knowledge of multi-level communication.

     3.   The practical avenues of communication.

     4.   If people get a clear picture of what could be, they will rally behind you and follow you.

II.   KEYS TO AN EFFECTIVE VISION STATEMENT

Type of Statement	What It Answers	Its Orientation
Purpose	Why does the church exist?	Theologically Oriented: What is the church's reason for being?
Vision	What is the church supposed to accomplish in ministry?	Seeing Oriented: What do we see in our heads as the vision is cast for us?
Mission	What is the church's ministry?	Objective Oriented: What does our plan look like?
Philosophy of Ministry	Why do we do what we do?	Value Oriented: What shapes our congregational culture?

A.   Concise wording

B.   Non-technical, easily grasped language

C.   Concise in concepts yet precise in wording

D.   Easy to remember

E.   Reflection of a biblical vision

III.   VISION STATEMENT EXAMINATION

A.   Examine the statement without destroying the statement

B.   A practical checklist
1.   Focused on the future?
2.   Clear and easily understandable?
3.   Brief?
4.   A reflection of God's vision, not yours?
5.   Identifying your distinctives?
6.   Inspiring to your congregation?
7.   Realistic but challenging?
8.   Fully owned by the senior pastor?
9.   Action-oriented?
10.   Biblically defensible?
11.   A potential rallying point?
12.   Focusing on a specific direction?
13.   Consistent with your mission?
14.   Consistent with your past?
15.   Strategic in nature?

IV.   VISION STATEMENT EXAMPLE OF WHAT TO DO AND NOT TO DO

A.   Vision Statement Example of What Not To Do
1.   "By the ordination of our omnipotent King, this ecclesiastical expression has been predestined to carry the oracle of divine reconciliation to our spiritually depraved and deprived peers."
2.   "We assertively enhance high-quality solutions as well as to collaboratively foster seven-habits-conforming information for 100% customer satisfaction."

B.   Vision Statement Example of What To Do
1.   City Bible Church
      • *Exalting the Lord* by dynamic, Holy Spirit inspired worship, praise and prayer. Giving our time, talents and gifts as an offering to the Lord.
      • *Equipping the church* to fulfill her destiny through godly vision, biblical teaching and pastoral ministries, bringing believers to maturity in Christ and effective ministry, resulting in a restored triumphant church.
      • *Extending the kingdom* of God through the church, to our city, our nation and the world through aggressive evangelism, training leaders, planting churches and sending missionaries and mission teams.

2.   Waverly Christian Fellowship: "To raise up fervent followers of Jesus Christ who will reach out and impact communities, cities and nations for the kingdom of God.

3.   Life Center
   - *Reaching* the hurting and the lost by caring, praying, bearing burdens and actively evangelizing
   - *Restoring* broken homes and lives with the washing and building up of God's Word
   - *Releasing* them to fulfill their God-given destiny

4.   Harvest International Ministries
   - To love and equip pastors in its association by providing fellowship, mutual support, conferences, and Ephesians 4:11 training
   - To help associated churches grow qualitatively and quantitatively
   - To assist associated churches in reaching the nations and fulfilling the Great Commission through church planting, particularly among the unreached people groups and in the 10/40 window.

5.   Willow Creek Community Church: "To turn irreligious people into fully devoted followers of Jesus Christ."

6.   New Life Church: "Our purpose is to know, worship and obey God according to the Scriptures. Our mission is to promote healthy relationships through small groups which empower people for ministry."

7.   Focus on the Family: To cooperate with the Holy Spirit in disseminating the Gospel of Jesus Christ to as many people as possible, and, specifically, to accomplish that objective by helping to preserve traditional values and the institution of the family.

8.   Church on the Way: We seek to teach the Word of God and spread the Gospel of Jesus Christ in the power of the Holy Spirit, shaping and equipping our church family so that believers will be nourished and empowered to fulfill their God-ordained, created purpose and ministry. We seek to prepare people who care for one another, and who sensitively reach to our City and our World that all may be saved, being brought to a living faith in Christ as Savior and Lord.

9.   People of Destiny Ministries: To proclaim God's grace, develop local churches, and influence our world with the gospel.

The Values & Ministry Philosophy of Vision

I. **VISION VALUES**
   (Sample from City Bible Church)

   A. *Value God's Word*. We believe that the Bible is God's inspired word, the authoritative and trustworthy rule of faith and practice for all Christians.

   B. *Value God's Manifested Presence.* To enjoy God's felt-realized presence is our passion as a church. We believe there is a presence of God available to God's people as they follow the pattern of worship as seen in the Psalms (Ps 22:3).

   C. *Value Holy Spirit Activity.* Both in our personal and corporate life as believers, we welcome the moving of the Holy Spirit. The baptism of the Holy Spirit and the gifts of the Holy Spirit are part of our basic belief system.

   D. *Value Dynamic Spontaneous Praise and Worship.* The believer's response to God's presence may be seen in the energetic worship with clapping, lifting hands and singing spontaneous unrehearsed songs unto the Lord.

   E. *Value the Principle of Unity.* Not conformity but unity of spirit and principle. Unity may express itself in a variety of ways but still maintain the same principles and convictions so as to flow together in accomplishing vision.

   F. *Value the Holiness of God.* Holiness is not legalism that is measured by outward look, but a true cleansing of the believer by the power of the Holy Spirit that is evidenced in Christian character and conduct. The fruit is easily born forth.

   G. *Value Fervent Prayer.* The voice of prayer is heard as we pray out loud together in our pre-service prayer times. This principle of prayer is believed to be the motor or powerhouse to our church life. Individual praying and fasting and prayer for the whole church is a continual emphasis.

   H. *Value Excellence.* We believe God deserves the best we have to offer; therefore we seek to maintain a high quality of excellence in everything connected to the work of God.

   I. *Value Relationships.* To love one another is our goal and we endeavor to make this practical through small groups called Life Groups, where every believer is encouraged to develop deeper relationships with other believers that result in encouragement and accountability.

J.   *Value Integrity*. There is no substitute for a lack in character. We hold this value in highest esteem and filter all other values through this one. Uprightness, trustworthiness and transparency are our best foundation stones.

K.   *Value Kingdom of God influence* in the culture we live. We are to be salt and light to our world. The political, the social and the educational penetrated by God's spirit and word.

L.   *Value the Family.* We express this commitment in our strong emphasis on family in preaching, teaching, available counseling, home school program and a K-12 Christian school.

II. GRASPING A CLEAR BIBLICAL MINISTRY PHILOSOPHY
(Mark 10:38; Luke 14:26-33; Mark 8:34)

A.   A philosophy of ministry that begins with a proper personal perspective for one's life, when self and all its rights and demands are truly nailed to the cross and the Lord becomes the center of one's existence.

B.   A philosophy of ministry that understands the doctrine of the Body of Christ, authority Vs submission and accountability. This means that the Body's health and protection override personal ambitions, hurts, offenses and trivial beliefs that might harm the Body.

C.   A philosophy that rises out of a personal encounter with God that results in a yielding to the call of God so that a biblical sacrifice relating to that call is demanded. Therefore, it is a joy and a privilege to give your life to training, discipleship, prayer and serving the Body.

D.   Potential Problem People (Acts 28:3)
      1.   People with conflicting views, opinions and concepts
      2.   People with hidden expectations or motivation
      3.   People with unsolved loyalties
      4.   People with a record of moral impurity
      5.   People with contentious, divisive spirits
      6.   People with a religious or letter-of-the-law spirit

The Discerning of Vision Destroyers

INTRODUCTION

The vision leader expects testing of the vision and attack upon the vision because that is the nature of vision. It gets attacked. It has enemies. It has testing. Vision can stand and grow through the testing or it can be destroyed. Vision is not only tested, but at times it can be limited. Some visions are limited by poor leadership, Satanic harassment or corrupted people.

I.   **VISION LIMITED BY LEADERSHIP**

      A.   Wrong Motivation

      B.   Unclear Perception (Hosea 7:11)

      C.   Self-willed

      D.   Small Minded (Joshua 17:14-18)

      E.   Fearful (Judges 6:11-17; 7:3)

      F.   Independent

      G.   Lazy (II Kings 13:14-19)

II.   **VISION LIMITED BY WRONG CONGREGATIONAL ATTITUDES**
      (Numbers 13:28 – 14:10)

      A.   Wrong Perspective

      B.   Wavering Faith

      C.   Grasshopper Complex

      D.   Retreat Mentality

      E.   Blameshifting

III.   **VISION LIMITED BY UNATTACKED STRONGHOLDS**
      (II Corinthians 10:3-4; II Chronicles 26:5-6)

      A.   The Stronghold of Eloth – Financial Limitations

B.　　The Stronghold of Gath – Human Impossibilities

C.　　The Stronghold of Jabneh – Satanic Harassment

D.　　The Stronghold of Ashdod – Immorality and Sexual Perversion

E.　　The Stronghold of Gurball – Humanism

F.　　The Stronghold of Mehumins – Religious Deception

G.　　The Stronghold of the Ammonites – Relational Conflicts

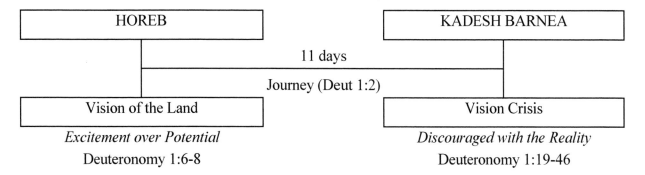

HOREB		KADESH BARNEA
	11 days	
	Journey (Deut 1:2)	
Vision of the Land		Vision Crisis

Excitement over Potential　　　　　　　　*Discouraged with the Reality*
Deuteronomy 1:6-8　　　　　　　　　　　　Deuteronomy 1:19-46

IV.　THE VISION DESTROYER OF WRONG FOCUS
(Numbers 13:28-33)

A.　　They magnify problems instead of magnifying the vision.

B.　　They magnify the power of the enemy instead of God's power.

C.　　They magnify negative words instead of faith words.

D.　　They distort their perception and believe in their distortion.

V.　THE PERSISTENT VISION DESTROYERS
(Nehemiah 2:20; 4:13)

A.　　Sanballet – Spirit of ridicule, irritation and harassment (Nehemiah 2:19; 4:7)

B.　　Tobiah – Spirit of betrayal (Nehemiah 4:3,7)

C.　　Noadiah – Spirit of false fear (Nehemiah 6:14)

D.　　Shemiah – Spirit of distraction (Nehemiah 6:10)

E.　　Geshem – Spirit of deception (Nehemiah 6:6)

The Seven Nevers of Vision

INTRODUCTION

The vision leader must draw a line in the sand—thus far and no further. There must be a "never do" list in all vision leader's mind. A commitment is made, a line is drawn, a "never" list begins. Here are seven nevers I have made and live by. You will add to these as your journey necessitates personal conviction nevers!

I.   Never allow the world, the flesh or the devil to shape your vision, for vision shapes destiny.

II.   Never allow smallness of vision to rule your life.
        (I Chronicles 4:9-10)

III.   Never allow those who have no faith to influence you.
        (Hebrews 11:1)

IV.   Never allow discouragement to dominate your faith in God fulfilling your vision.
        (Micah 7:7-8)

V.   Never allow circumstances to limit your vision; change your circumstances through faith.
(Isaiah 50:11)

VI.   Never allow finances to become the dictator to the vision. God is your resource.

VII. Never allow failure to set your course in life. Get up again, try again, never give up!
(Micah 7:7-8)

The Distinctives of a Prophetic People

I Corinthians 10:1-13; Exodus 1-25; Ezra 5:1-2; Haggai 2:4; Ezra 3:2,10

INTRODUCTION

A prophetic people are a people who maintain a cutting edge in attitude and ministry by moving consistently forward in fulfilling their God-given received mission. The work or vision of God is greatly influenced by the prophetic word and the prophetic spirit. Prophetic ministry ignites vision expectation and encourages people to see beyond the unfinished vision, beyond the broken down walls and ruins. The prophetic ministry stirs people to have faith and hope to see the vision fulfilled.

DISTINCTIVE 1

Those who have spiritually and theologically grasped the biblically stated eternal purpose of God. (Ephesians 3:10-11; Genesis 1:26-28; Matthew 16:16-18)

DISTINCTIVE 2

Those who have spiritually and enthusiastically committed themselves to the declared mission of their local church. (Proverbs 29:18; Habakkuk 2:2; Philippians 3:13-14)

DISTINCTIVE 3

Those who by spiritual warfare protect the mission, defeat the enemy and fulfill God's eternal purpose. (Ephesians 6:10-17; Ezra 4:21-24)

DISTINCTIVE 4

Those who by wisdom work out a simple strategy to accomplish a complex mission. (Proverbs 24:1-3; Ezra 5:8; 6:14)

DISTINCTIVE 5

Those who have nurtured a spirit of faith that lays hold of mission advancement. (I Corinthians 10:10; Exodus 1-15; Acts 7:38)

The Principles of Vision Advancement

INTRODUCTION
Vision is a spiritual force that, once imparted to the people of God, becomes a mighty power to move the church forward. The forward movement of the church is a sign of life, just as no movement is a sign of spiritual stagnation and ultimately spiritual death. The principles of vision advancement are vital to the vision leader, especially when movement has been hindered or is stopped completely. An advancement spirit must first be in the vision leader before it can be imparted to the people.

I. **THREE ADVANCEMENT PROPOSITIONS**

    A.   The church was never meant to have a survival mentality

    B.   The church is meant to be triumphant, militant and victorious.
        1. The church is to have the attitude of Jonathan (I Samuel 14:6)
        2. The church is to have the attitude of Caleb (Joshua 14:12)
        3. The church is to have the attitude of David (I Samuel 17:48)

    C.   The church is always to advance and move forward by the power of the Holy Spirit.

II. **FOUR LESSONS FROM THE CHURCH IN THE WILDERNESS**
(I Corinthians 10:11-13)

    A.   Israel's experience is a type.

    B.   Israel's experience is an admonition to us.

    C.   Israel's experience is relevant to our day.

    D.   Israel's experience is a prophetic warning.

III. **EXODUS: THE BOOK OF ADVANCEMENT**

    A.   Historical Setting of Exodus

Genesis	Exodus
Biography	History
Fortunes of a family	Growth into a nation
Promise	Fulfillment

    B.   Advancement in Exodus

IV.   ADVANCEMENT PRINCIPLES

A.   God's eternal purpose has never changed.   It is progressive from generation to generation. (Exodus 1:1-7; 2:24-25)

B.   God's true people have always endured cultures, governments and persecutions while advancing in every generation. (Exodus 1:8-22)

C.   God has always had His prophetic leaders being secretly prepared for God's prophetic moments. (Exodus 2:1 – 4:17; Isaiah 49:1-3)

D.   Every people that advances in mission together must establish spiritual bonding with God's chosen leadership. (Exodus 4:18 – 6:27)

E.   God's people always confront a pharaohistic culture with its many false gods and false powers (Exodus 7:1 – 12:29)

F.   Vision advancement is initiated by God. (Exodus 12:39)

G.   Vision advancement is successful when the divine timing of God is recognized. (Genesis 15:16; Exodus 12:40)

H.   Vision advancement is accomplished by the power and strength of God. (Exodus 13:14)

I.   Vision advancement is carrying the bones of Joseph, past faithful visionaries. (Exodus 13:19; Hebrews 11:22)

J.   Vision advancement begins with small steps of obedience and faith. (Exodus 13:20)

K.   Vision advancement is realizing the Lord is moving ahead of us to make way. (Exodus 13:21)

L.   Vision advancement is the willingness to experience divine entrapment. (Exodus 14:1-3)

M.   Vision advancement provokes the enemy to attack and become aggressive. (Exodus 14:5)

N.   Vision advancement exposes our heart, our faith, our trust. (Exodus 14:10)

O.   Vision advancement is accomplished when we see crisis as dangerous opportunities. (Exodus 14:13)

P.   Vision advancement is made possible by understanding prophetic seasons. (Exodus 14:15)

Q.   Vision advancement happens when every obstacle is overcome by breaking through. (Exodus 14:16)

R. Vision advancement will glorify God as one who is able to defeat all the enemies.
(Exodus 14:17)

S. Vision advancement will affect our attitude toward God as we see His works.
(Exodus 14:28)

T. Vision advancement will result in victorious, triumphant worship.
(Exodus 15:1-3)

U. Vision advancement must successfully overcome wilderness hazards.
(Exodus 15:22-26)

V. Vision advancement will result in building the house of God.
(Exodus 25:1-10)

W Vision advancement will result in possessing all of the vision through unified warfare.
(Joshua 1-15)

The Power of Vision Momentum

INTRODUCTION: Vision needs momentum in order to fulfill God's purpose for His people. Momentum is the power of the Holy Spirit in action, causing the church to be righteously stimulated to arise and fulfill the vision. Momentum is evidenced by joy, expectation, zeal, bold worship and a willingness to work together. Momentum is like a mighty wave that carries all that are in it by the power and movement of the wave. Spiritually advancing people are those who maintain a cutting edge in attitude and ministry by moving consistently forward in fulfilling their God-given received mission.

> Spiritual advancement is the process by which God moves a willing people continually forward toward their spiritual destiny, creating spiritual momentum that is maintained through spiritual warfare.

I. MOMENTUM AND THE MOVER

Momentum = the creating of movement, force or motion

Mover = one who moves or sets something in motion

A.   The Mover is a

B.   Obstacles Movers Encounter
(Joshua 1:1-2; Isaiah 40:3; 57:14; 62:10; Luke 5:38-39)

   1.   The obstacle of letting the old die to bring in the new

   2.   The obstacle of letting go of non-productive leadership/staff

   3.   The obstacles of traditional church ideas

   4.   The obstacle of past failures or victories

   5.   The obstacle of influential people with poor attitudes

   6.   The obstacle of past record of poor decision making

II. THE SOURCE OF MOMENTUM

A.   The External Sovereign Force

B.   The Internal Principle Force

III. THE CHEMISTRY OF LOCAL CHURCH MOMENTUM

A. The Spiritual Climate
   1. Holy Spirit Prayer
   2. Corporate Gathering
   3. Conflict Minimized
   4. Faith Level High
   5. Spiritual Warfare

B. The Leadership Cohesiveness

> Management of Vision = Manner in which individuals fit and blend together without losing their uniqueness or individuality.

   1. Unity of Spirit (I Corinthians 1:10; Psalm 133)
   2. Unity of Sacrifice
   3. Unity of Philosophy
      a. Worship
      b. Prayer
      c. Music
      d. Visitors
      e. Evangelism
      f. Preaching
      g. Corporate Gathering
      h. Meeting the Needs of People
      i. Leadership
      j. Tithes and Offerings
      k. Spiritual Gifts
      l. Small Groups
      m. Christian Education
      n. Christian School
      o. Church Growth

C. The Structural Preparation
   1. The bones factor
   2. The communication factor
   3. The flexibility factor
   4. The right people in right places factor

D. The Position of the People Through Preaching
   1. Feeding to prepare hearts to receive
   2. Feeding to cultivate faith attitude that rises to challenge
   3. Feeding to establish vision values
   4. Feeding to arouse expectation

E. The Congregational Awareness of Vision

The Momentum Killers

I.   **MOMENTUM: A PRECIOUS COMMODITY TO GUARD**

II.   **MOMENTUM KILLERS**

     A.   The Galatian Church Destroyer: Legalism

     B.   The Corinthian Church Destroyer: Mixture Tolerated
            (I Corinthians 5)

     C.   The Jerusalem Church Destroyer: Structural Strangulation
            (Acts 6:1)

     D.   The Ephesian Church Destroyer: Lukewarmness

     E.   The Saul Church Destroyer: Faulty Senior Leader

     F.   The Solomon Church Destroyer: Success Mishandled

     G.   The Laodicean Church Destroyer: Pride/Self-Deception

The Hub and Spoke Tension of Vision

I.   DEFINING THE HUB AND SPOKES

A.   The Hub – The basic, biblical vision (non-negotiable)

The hub represents the theological, unchangeable, basic doctrines of the Bible which become the foundation for the church's mission statements, purpose, vision and destiny, out of which all strategies are built.

Rim

Spokes

Hub

B.   The Spokes – The extended vision (negotiable)
(Isaiah 65:8)

The spokes represent the unchangeable principles which become the expressions of truth in principle statements, precepts, concepts and philosophy.

1.   Principle: Comes from the word "prince" or "first". It can signify precepts, respected methods of operation or guidelines which shape an organization. A principle is a guiding force, a comprehensive and fundamental law, doctrine or assumption.

2.   Principles that build churches that last[1]
   a.   The dynamic hub
   b.   The objective rules the subjective
   c.   The clear interprets the obscure
   d.   The major emphasis rules the minor
   e.   Proven basics come before unproven success ideas
   f.   The principle of the cross
   g.   The team principle
   h.   The biblical vision mandate

---

[1]Frank Damazio. Keys to Successful Leadership (Portland, Oregon: City Bible Publishing).

C.   The Rim

The rim represents the changeable styles, procedures and ideas for applying and communicating truth to the present times and culture. It represents the methods whereby truth is applied.

II.   POTENTIAL IMBALANCE PROBLEMS BETWEEN HUB AND SPOKES

To allow the church to become fragmented by allowing any one spoke to be disconnected from the hub.

A.   Potential Spoke Problems

1.   Forgetting the hub as the source of the spoke

2.   Allowing a single spoke to become the major focus of the church until it shrouds the hub

3.   The danger of fragmentation due to decentralization and departmentalization
    a.   This could also be called institutionalization. In this case the spokes would become their own hubs [sub-hubs].
    b.   The underlying truths that form the hub must be constantly repeated in the spokes. We must remember that the spokes are means, not ends. In all areas our motivation must be a love for the House of the Lord.

B.   Danger signals that indicate a spoke is becoming alienated from the hub:
    1.   Attendance at the corporate gathering; imbalanced attendance as compared to spoke events.
    2.   A superior attitude in a department (or individual in the department).
    3.   An imbalanced personal doctrinal emphasis in the department.
    4.   A critical attitude toward the senior leadership.
    5.   The use of "we/they" language.

    6.   A loss of first love for Christ and His house.
    7.   An inability to relate to the hub as well as to a spoke.
    8.   An imbalanced emphasis on personal or departmental ministry; "empire building" or too much tunnel vision in the leadership of a spoke.
    9.   Inconsistent stewardship, especially as seen in giving to the hub as compared to giving to the spoke.
    10. An imbalanced promotion of a spoke and its agenda.
    11. A defensive attitude in the leadership of a spoke.
    12. The development of a personality cult around the leader of a spoke.
    13. Redirection of personal affection and empowerment from the hub to a spoke.
    14. A lack of participation in corporate hub prayer.

15. Poor communication from the leader of a spoke to the leader of the hub, poor accountability.
16. Poor discipleship of new believers as a result of not plugging them into the hub.
17. Poor articulation of the basic vision from department leaders to the members of their department.
18. A lack of involvement in spokes other than ones own.
19. Poor involvement in hub worship times.
20. A desire for the financial independence of the spoke.

C. Ways to Avoid These Imbalances
1. Cross-departmental activities.
2. A basic commitment on the part of all leaders to strengthen the hub.
3. A commitment to all the spokes contributing to the hub.
4. Consistent communication of the basic vision in the corporate gatherings.
5. More emphasis on the basic vision in the church life classes.
6. Being open to input from other departments.
7. Department heads being open to these danger signals.
8. Bathing the articulation of the vision in love and caring.
9. More involvement of the departments in the corporate gatherings.
10. A spirit of loyalty among the leaders.
11. The physical presence of senior leadership in departmental activities.
12. Prayer for the needs of other departments in departmental staff meetings.
13. Communication of departmental activities to all the leadership.
14. The senior pastor should regularly meet with the heads of his spokes.

Vision for a Church that Understands Revival

I. THE GREAT AWAKENING: TWO GROUPS

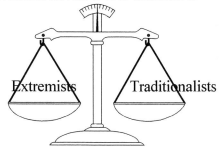

A. Jonathan Edward's Test of Authenticity
1. True revival raises the esteem of Jesus in the community, preaching Him as scripture depicts Him: Son of God and Savior.
2. True revival works against the Kingdom of Satan which encourages sin and worldly lusts.
3. True revival stimulates a greater regard for the Holy Scriptures and establishes them more in their truth and divinity.
4. True revival is marked by a spirit of truth.
5. True revival manifests a renewed love of God and of man.

B. Insights from Historical Revivals
1. Revivals are seemingly messy by nature. The Holy Spirit moves within a human environment that is always molded by sin, including encumbering religious traditions and demonic presences.
2. Revival manifestations of the Holy Spirit are imperfect and contaminated because of human involvement and human response to Holy Spirit presence.
3. Revival activities, beliefs and behaviors should be spiritually discerned: not discerned by one's emotional opinions, religious background or personal likes or dislikes; but discerned based on biblical principles.
4. Revivals are God's design to "dig the wells of refreshing," to unblock these wells by removing all the rocks of wrong traditions, wrong theology, wrong ideas that have kept God's people from the pure water in the well,

II. PORTRAIT OF A CHURCH IN REVIVAL

A. A church that experiences the power proclamation and demonstration of the Gospel. (I Thessalonians 1:5-6)

B.   A church that resists the continuous infiltration of an idolatrous culture.
         (I Thessalonians 1:9)

C.   A church that is not shaken by faith's apparent contradictions.
         (I Thessalonians 3:2-5)

D.   A church that makes personal holiness a serious objective, especially sexual purity.
         (I Thessalonians 3:13; 4:1-8)

E.   A church that encourages true spirituality as seen in a person's work ethic.
         (I Thessalonians 4:9-12)

F.   A church that wisely follows proven leadership.
         (I Thessalonians 5:12-13)

G.   A church that clearly pursues biblical wholeness for each individual in a defined
         biblical process.
         (I Thessalonians 5:23-24)

H.   A church that establishes doctrine as the foundation, not religious trends, emotional
         spiritual experiences or charismatic personalities.
         (II Thessalonians 1:5-12; 2:10-11)

I.   A church that guards against spiritual gullibility that creeps in when subjective
         experiences are exalted above objective truth.
         (II Thessalonians 2:9-17)

III.   PAULINE COUNSEL TO A CHURCH IN REVIVAL

A.   I Thessalonians 5:19-21

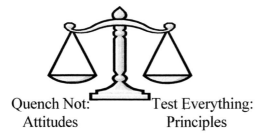

Quench Not: Test Everything:
Attitudes   Principles

B.   Respect and Cooperate with the Holy Spirit

1.   "Quench not the Spirit." (I Thessalonians 5:19)
"Believers must also be careful not to quench, suppress or extinguish the fire of the Spirit."
"Stop putting out the Spirit's fire."
"Quench not the manifestations of the Spirit."

2.   Quench (Gr) = to extinguish or quench, to suppress, subdue, stifle, to snuff out, stamp out, cause something to dry up (Matthew 12:20; 25:8; Mark 9:44-48; Ephesians 4:16; I Thessalonians 5:19; Hebrews 11:34)

IV.   TESTING THE AUTHENTICITY OF REVIVAL
I Thessalonians 5:21
"...All things however, test..."
"...And yet you must scrutinize it all carefully..."
"...By all means, use your judgement and hold on to whatever is good."

A.   The Word "Test"

1.   The Old Testament Hebrew
   a.   Nasah: Indicates the attempt to prove the quality of someone or something; often a time of pressure and difficulty constitutes the test. (Exodus 16:4; 20:20; Deuteronomy 8:16; Judges 2:22)
   b.   Sarap: Means to smelt or refine and refers to the process by which gold or silver is refined; used to illustrate the purification process of God's people. (Jeremiah 6:27-30; Ezekiel 22:18-22; Psalm 17:3; 26:2; Isaiah 48:10)
   c.   Bahan: To test specifically in the spiritual realm with a focus on some quality such as integrity. It has the sense of examination designed to prove the existence of quality sought. (Genesis 42:15-16; I Chronicles 29:17; Job 7:18; Psalm 7:9; Proverbs 17:3; Malachi 3:10-11)

2.   The New Testament Greek
   a.   Dokimazo, dokime, dokimos: Words in this family emphasize that the test is designed to display the genuiness of that which is tried. Accepted as trustworthy and acknowledged as authentic. (Romans 12:2; 16:10; I Corinthians 3:13; II Corinthians 2:9; Galatians 6:4; I Timothy 3:10; I John 4:1)
   b.   Anakrino: To examine, to investigate, used of searching or enquiry carefully. (Acts 17:11; I Corinthians 9:3; 10:25-27)

B.   The Testing Applied Practically

1.   The testing process should salvage the good and discard the useless.

2.   The testing process should eliminate the dross and recover the valuable or genuine hidden parts.

3.   The testing process necessitates using your mind to think clearly by examining closely the basic theologies that undergird spiritual claims and subjective experiences.

C.   The Believer's Principles for Testing

1.   The Principle of Holding the Written Word as Supreme
       (I John 4:1; Acts 2:42; I Timothy 5:17; II Timothy 4:2)

       a.   Possibility of Deception (Jeremiah 29:8; Matthew 24:4; Ephesians 5:6; I Timothy 4:1; I Thessalonians 2:4; Romans 2:2)

       b.   Proper Placement of the Written Word of God (Hebrews 6:18-19; Psalm 19:7-10)

2.   The Principle of Fruit Examination
       (Matthew 7:16; John 16:2-8; 15:16; Philippians 1:11; Hebrews 12:11)

       a.   Spiritual phenomena from God have certain distinguishable characteristics. (Galatians 5:19-21; I Peter 1:5-10)

       b.   Spiritual experiences taking place inwardly must grow to outward visibility. (Jude 12; Matthew 13:22; Mark 4:19)

       c.   What would be the fruit of people touched by revival?

3.   The Principle of Discerning a Shift in Focus and Perspective
       (Matthew 17:1-7)

       a.   Spiritual experiences must be absorbed and then channeled properly.

       b.   Spiritual encounters with God always cause a biblical shift in our focus.

The Vision and Spiritual Warfare

> Vision is that which a congregation perceives by the Holy Spirit as pertaining to God's purpose for them, thereby creating spiritual momentum resulting in spiritual advancement and maintained through spiritual warfare.

Proclamation Process	Vision Visibility	Vision Established
"Word" Stage	"Warfare" Stage	"Vanguard" Stage
Prophetic Word	Weapons of War	Watchman Alert

I.   THE POWER COMPLEX

A. Two ages stand in conflict with one another. One is the kingdom of darkness, sin and death; demonic powers govern it. The other is a kingdom of life and righteousness and Christ governs it. (Ephesians 6:11-12; Colossians 1:16; 2:15)

B. Entangled network of forces that work simultaneously attacking God's proclaimed plan. These forces work continually upon the minds of all (believers and unbelievers), changing people's values, harassing the church, and are persistent in destroying godly people.

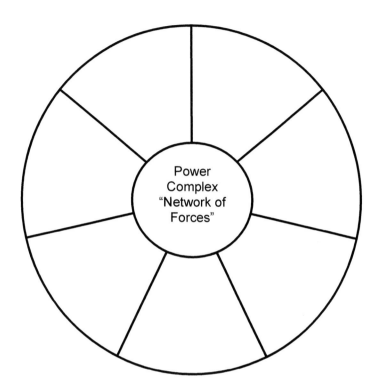

II. THE WARFARE STAGE OF THE VISION
Spiritual warfare is a time of warring with proven weapons to defeat the enemy and establish the purposes of God, fulfilling God-given vision with Holy Spirit determination.

A. Know Your Enemy
(II Corinthians 2:11; Ephesians 6:11; Genesis 49:22)

1. Satan always seeks to usurp authority
(Isaiah 14:12-15; Ezekiel 28:11-17)

2. Satan will twist truth into a partial lie in order to deceive.
(Genesis 3:1-5; John 8:44; II Corinthians 11:3; Revelation 12:9)

3. Satan attacks the family, the body and our possessions.
(Job 1:6)

4. Satan attacks with condemnation.
(Zechariah 3:1-6)

5. Satan wars against our prayers.
(Daniel 10:13,20)

6. Satan tempts man by appealing to the natural appetites.
(I Corinthians 7:5; I Timothy 5:15)

7. Satan fills the heart with wickedness.
(Acts 5:1-6; Proverbs 4:20-23)

8. Satan fills the mind with wrong words.
(Matthew 16:23; Romans 12:1-3; Philippians 4:1-3; Romans 8:6-7; II Corinthians 4:4; Proverbs 23:7)

9. Satan snatches away good seed. He is a thief.
(Mark 4:15; John 10:10; Matthew 13:19)

10. Satan desires to have you sift you as wheat.
(Luke 22:31)

11. Satan entered into Judas.
(Luke 22:3; John 13:27)

12. Satan can destroy a life.
(I Corinthians 5:5; I Timothy 1:20)

13. Satan seeks to take advantage.
(II Corinthians 2:11)

14.   Satan transforms himself into an angel of light.
        (II Corinthians 11:14)

15.   Satan desires to buffet servants of God.
        (II Corinthians 12:7)

16.   Satan desires to hinder the purposes and plans of God's people.
        (I Thessalonians 2:18)

17.   Satan seeks a place to rule, to establish a false throne.
        (Revelation 2:13)

18.   Satan desires to oppress the people of God.
        (Matthew 17:15; Acts 10:38)

19.   Satan desires to take spiritual ground from the believer and build strongholds.
        (Ephesians 4:17)

20.   Satan desires to render people useless by binding them.
        (Luke 13:16; Judges 6:5,19,22)

21.   Satan blinds the minds of the unbeliever.
        (II Corinthians 4:4)

B.   Declare War on the Enemy of Your Vision
        (Proverbs 20:18; Isaiah 54:17; Deuteronomy 28:7)

C.   Give the Enemy No Place to Hinder Your Vision
        (Ephesians 4:32; I John 1:1-5)

Vision Leprosy
Removing Spiritual Leprosy from the Vision

I.   REMOVE THE LEPROSY OF PRIDE: UZZIAH

A.   Definitions

    1.   Pride: an exaggerated idea of one's importance; arrogant behavior or conduct

    2.   Conceit: an exaggerated estimate of one's own ability

    3.   Egotistical: given to talking about one's self

B.   Results of pride

    1.   Dishonor (Proverbs 11:2)

    2.   Strife (Proverbs 13:10)

    3.   Destruction and stumbling (Proverbs 16:18)

    4.   Controversy (Proverbs 28:25)

C.   Identifying pride in our life

    1.   Pride focuses on gaining power

    2.   Pride puts emphasis on freedom instead of responsibility

    3.   Pride is concerned with gain, not giving

    4.   Pride desires immediate fulfillment instead of lasting achievement.

    5.   Pride yearns for the praise of men instead of God's approval.

    6.   Pride needs to be served instead of serving others.

    7.   Pride feeds on self-gratification not self-control.

    8.   Pride pushes ahead without preparation instead of having patience.

    9.   Pride loves competition not cooperation.

II.   REMOVE THE LEPROSY OF GREED: GEHAZI

A.   Gehazi (Heb): Valley of vision.
(II Kings 5:15-27)

B.   Greed : To hunger for something, reaching forward, eager to obtain something, strong desire.

C.   Greed caused by carelessness

    1.   Carelessness with his heart, not guarding from common sin (II Ki 5:20-21)

    2.   Carelessness with his relationship to God, to truth and honesty (II Ki 5:22)

    3.   Carelessness with his appreciation and esteem for the mantle

    4.   Carelessness with his desires, not disciplined or bringing his body under (II Kings 5:26; I Corinthians 9:25-27)

D.   Humility: The key to cleansing
       (Luke 4:27; II Kings 5:8-14)

E.   Scriptures pertaining to greed: Job 31:24; Psalm 119:36; Proverbs 15:27; Proverbs
       21:25; Proverbs 23:4; Matthew 6:19-21; 6:24-25

III.   REMOVE THE LEPROSY OF THE TONGUE: MIRIAM
       (Numbers 12:1-16)

A.   Power of the Tongue
       (James 3:5)

       1.   Destroys friendships (Proverbs 17:9; 16:28)

       2.   Destroys the harmony of the church (Romans 16:17; Proverbs 26:22)

       3.   Destroys loyalty (Numbers 12:1-10; I Corinthians 13:5-6)

       4.   Destroys the health of the body (Proverbs 26:22)

       5.   Destroys the edification in the body (Ephesians 4:29)

       6.   Destroys the purity of the body (James 3:1-12)

B.   Tongue Snares and Sins that Cause Leprosy

       1.   Whisperer: One who secretly passes on evil reports to others. (Psalm 41:7)

       2.   Gossip: One who magnifies and sensationalizes rumors and partial
              information

       3.   Slanderer: One who seeks to destroy another's credibility or reputation with
              damaging facts or evil suspicions. (Numbers 14:36; Psalm 101:5)

       4.   Busybody: One who digs up evil reports and makes it his business to spread
              them. (I Peter 4:15)

       5.   Railer: One who causes division with his tongue. (I Timothy 5:14; I Peter
              3:9; I Corinthians 5:11; 6:10)

       6.   Murmuring: those who confer together secretly and discontentedly complain
              to others who are powerless to change the situation; (I Corinthians 10:10;
              Proverbs 15:4; Ephesians 4:29; Philippians 2:14; Acts 6:1)

C.   Cleansing the Leprous House
       (Leviticus 14:49)

       1.   New Freedom

       2.   New Sensitivity

       3.   New Life Dependent upon Holy Spirit Grace

       4.   New Love Ministry

Vision Warning
Building Without Blessing

It is immediately apparent that Psalm 127 emphasizes the need of divine blessing for all undertakings. It conveys this lesson with unmistakable clearness and clear emphasis. This psalm is especially written for the builders of God's House, the church, the people of the Lord. We are taught here that builders of houses, cities, fortune, empires and churches all labor in vain without the Lord. But under divine favor they find sweet and restful success. This psalm points out clearly man's need of the genuine blessing of the Almighty. Spurgeon calls this Psalm "The Builder's Psalm" or "The Psalm directed against self-reliance." A German proverb states, "Everything depends on God's blessing." This Psalm can represent our life, our family, or our church. (Matthew 7:24-27; I Corinthians 3:5-15; Matthew 16:18; I Chronicles 28:20; II Chronicles 5:13)

Solomon (I Kings 3:5-15; II Chronicles 2:1-9; 3:1; 5:1; 6:40-42; 7:11-16)

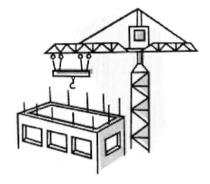

I.   THE POSSIBILITY OF BUILDING WITHOUT BLESSING

A.   "Unless" – A Word of Divine Warning
(Matthew 12:29; 18:3; 24:22; Jn 3:3)

B.   Builders Who Built Without Divine Direction and Blessing

1.   The Babel Model (Genesis 11:4-8)

2.   The Jeroboam Model (I Kings 12:25-33)

II.   THE POSSIBILITY OF BUILDING IN VAIN
(Psalm 127:1)

A.   Builders Useless Labor – "They labor in vain who build it"

B.   Identifying Labor That is in Vain

III.   THE POSSIBILITY OF BUILDING SUCCESSFULLY WITHOUT STRAIN
(Psalm 127:2)

A.   The Sleep that God rewards

B. Identifying Spiritual Strain – success of God without strain

    1. Sense of inadequacy

    2. Attitude of anxiety

    3. Condition of fear

    4. Wrong perspective and attitude toward others

    5. Spiritual depression

    6. Promotion confusion

IV. THE POSSIBILITY OF BUILDING WITH DIVINE BLESSING

A. **The Blessing of the Lord Examined**
(Genesis 1:22; 49:25-26; Proverbs 10:22; Genesis 1:26-28; Psalm 3:8; 24:5; Deuteronomy 28:2)
Blessing (Hebrew) = "to endue with power for success, prosperity, longevity, provision, protection, glory, honor, favor"

B. **Acquiring the Blessing of the Lord**
Abundant life enriched by God is to be found in the Lord's available covenant of Grace and practically experienced as we obey His word, walk in His ways.

    1. Blessing acquired by covenant with God
(Genesis 12:2-3; 17:16; Galatians 3:14; Psalm 32:1; Romans 15:29; Ephesians 1:3)

    2. Blessing acquired by maintaining integrity and purity of focus
(Psalm 24:4-5; Psalm 119:1-2; Proverbs 10:6)

    3. Blessing acquired by rejecting the temptation of human power
(Psalm 1:1; I Corinthians 2:1-16)

    4. Blessing acquired by cultivating a healthy understanding of God – learning to fear the Lord
(Psalm 112:1; Proverbs 22:4; Psalm 128:1)

    5. Blessing acquired by guarding harmony with a passion
(I Corinthians 1:20; Mark 3:24-25; Psalm 133:1-3)

    6. Blessing acquired by treating fragmentations as devilish
(Psalm 133:1-3; Isaiah 65:8; Daniel 2:31-45)

7. Blessing acquired by always being liberal
   (Ezekiel 44:30; Malachi 3:10)

8. Blessing acquired by exalting faithfulness, never flashiness
   (Proverbs 28:20)

9. Blessing acquired by dealing with attitudes, not just actions
   (Matthew 5:3-16; Luke 6:20-22)

10. Blessing acquired by cleansing offenses often
    (I Corinthians 10:16)

11. Blessing acquired by learning the truth of brokenness
    (I Corinthians 4:10)

12. Blessing acquired by attaining true wisdom
    (Proverbs 8:32-36; James 3:13-18; Isaiah 55:10-11)

13. Blessing acquired by grace and spirit, not by might and power
    (Zechariah 4:4-6; Exodus 33:14-15; II Corinthians 12:10)

14. Blessing acquired by following God's pattern, not man's ideas
    (Acts 26:19; Exodus 40:32-34; I Chronicles 28:11-12)

Pulling Down Vision Strongholds

I. STRONGHOLDS

    A.   Negativism

    B.   Stronghold of maintenance mentality

    C.   Stronghold of status quo

    D.   Stronghold of city principalities

    E.   Stronghold of religious unbelief

    F.   Always Be Spiritually Alert to Vision Attackers

II. WEAPONS OF WARFARE TO PROTECT YOUR VISION

    A.   Weapon of Fervent Prayer
            (Joshua 8:18,26)

B. Weapon of Praise
    (Psalm 149-150)

C. Weapon of the Blood
    (Revelation 12:11)

D. Weapon of Our Confession
    (Revelation 12:11)

E. Weapon of Resistance
    (I Peter 5:8-9; James 4:7)

F. Weapon of Exposing the Enemy's Tactics

Safe Search for Successful Church Models

INTRODUCTION

We must understand the times in which we serve as leaders and the context of our ministry challenges. As we recognize the astronomical changes seen in culture worldwide, we must intensify our search for appropriate forms, structures, styles, programs and ministry philosophy that rise to the occasion. In our search, we must sustain certain biblical truths that make up our spiritual distinctives, our convictions. To focus on people more than programs and process more than structure is one of many "now" challenges. Our desire is to march into the 21st century, not to stumble in organizational darkness. Our desire is not to be movements representing what used to be, but mission starters designed to meet the future. We all have a choice: to be a historical church or a history-making church.

Presupposition: Successful churches are difficult to find, to build and to sustain; therefore our desire must be intense and our journey must be disciplined.

I.   SUCCESSFUL CHURCHES BIBLICALLY EVALUATED

A.   New Testament Standard
(Matthew 16:16-18)

B.   New Testament Models
(Acts 2:37-47; 15; 20; Revelation 1-7)

II.   SUCCESSFUL CHURCHES HISTORICALLY EVALUATED

A.   Cultural Impact: Did they penetrate the people of their day?

B.   Longevity of Fruitfulness: Did they leave a legacy?

C.   Adherence to Basic Orthodoxy: Did they use biblical truth?

III. SUCCESSFUL CHURCHES IN OUR TIMES

A. Variety of Success Models

    1. Vineyard

    2. Hybels

    3. Cell-churches

    4. Mainline denominational

    5. Charismatic

    6. MFI or restoration churches

B. Successful Churches Are Still Changing (no definite model)

C. Ecclesiology Runs Out of Our Theology (spiritual roots)

D. Danger of:

    1. Exclusivism

    2. Judgmental spirit

    3. Rigid criticism without the facts

IV. SEARCHING FOR SUCCESS TRUTHS, PRINCIPLES AND METHODS

A. Search scripture first.

B. Be aware of potential extremes in your search.

C.   Don't commit intellectual suicide. Learn, read, take extended education classes.

D.   Learn some discernment factors.

Questions to ask:
1.   Has it been proven yet for any length of time?
2.   Who of spiritual stature endorses this?
3.   What obvious problems do you see? Have they been explained?
4.   Does it violate your basic understanding of New Testament success components of the church?
5.   What do you have to give up to have this kind of church? Is it worth it?

V.   LEADERSHIP JOURNEY IN BUILDING SUCCESSFUL CHURCHES

A.   The New Testament Model Factor
Clear perspective of New Testament components for successful churches

B.   The Leadership Factor

1.   The leader's level of seriousness

2.   The leader's level of gifting

3.   The leader's level of discipleship

4.   The leader's level of spiritual depth

5.   The leader's level of wisdom

C.   The Vision Factor

D.   The Structure and Strategy Factor

1.   Transformation

2.   Mobilization

3.   Lay ministry programs

E. The Bride Building Factor

   1. Church in culture: relevancy issue

   2. Church in culture: evangelism issue

   3. Church in culture: racism issue

   4. Church in culture: five generations issue

F. The Corporate Gathering Factor

   1. Worship styles: biblically based worship and culturally relevant

   2. Preaching styles: great debates over what is right for today

   3. Time element: a cultural hazard must be evaluated

   4. Philosophy of church service

      a. Is it biblical?

      b. Is it too narrow?

      c. When did you get it?

Vision for a Church with a Committed Membership

Introduction: Church membership is a step into partnership, a partnership in vision. Through the membership class, vision is imparted to the believer and they become an active partner of the church and the vision. Membership is a synonym for building committed believers into a committed local church. The content, length of classes, and method of teaching may vary but the principle of building unity of vision and commitment is needed in every church.

I. GOAL OF MEMBERSHIP—A HEALTHY MEMBER

> **Healthy Member Profile:** The goal of our ministry to every member is to help them to become a person who is born again, water baptized and filled with the Spirit, who is faithful to the corporate church gatherings, cell ministry and School of Equipping; joyfully gives their tithe, enjoys prayer and worship, has a heart for winning our city to Christ and a vision for world missions, upholds family values and loves God with all their heart, soul, mind and strength.

II. SAMPLE STRUCTURE OF A NEW MEMBERS CLASS

A. Qualifications to Become a Member of City Bible Church

 1. Must be born again.
 2. Must be 18 years of age.
 3. Must complete a New Member's Class
 4. Must have completely filled out a Membership Application Form (a blue card)
 5. Must have walked forward in a membership induction service, and verbally made a membership commitment to the elders of the church.
 6. Must attend a Cell group

B. Class Schedule

 1. Each class is # weeks long and is held on either a Sunday morning before second service or on a Wednesday night. The class member cannot miss more than four lessons and must complete the missed lessons via tape before they graduate the course.
 2. Each class begins with a time of fellowship and then a time of prayer.

C.   Weekly Class

    1.   Each week the class consists of specific components:
        a.   Pre-class prayer by the teaching team
        b.   Opening with a worship chorus and prayer
        c.   Teaching the lesson
        d.   Fellowship
        e.   Prayer and ministry time

    2.   When a lesson is taught, opportunities are given in that class to begin practicing what has been taught as various opportunities either to minister or to become involved in the church are offered:
        a.   Personal growth: Praying for salvation or the baptism of the Holy Spirit; Sign up for water baptism
        b.   Ministry involvement: Volunteer for a ministry such as Stitches or guest ministries.
        c.   Church involvement: Sign up for a cell group
        d.   Implementing what was taught that week: Partaking of communion at the end of the lesson on communion, worshipping at the end of the lesson on worship

    3.   Strategically building relationships with each person before and after class each week.

D.   New Member's Care
    1.   The goal of New Member's Care is contacting each New Member and to pastor and care for them. Many of them are new to the church and have no other means of contact with any of the Pastoral staff. For many in the class, the teacher is the only pastor they know and that is involved in their lives; therefore the instructor must build relationship with them, praying for their needs, and taking a general interest in their lives through contacting them on a regular basis.
    2.   The teacher calls each class member on a regular basis, at least every other week using the New Member's Care Report and the Assimilation Report. This assists in pastoring each person individually.

E.   New Member's Follow Up
    1.   The goal of following up with each New Member's class attendee is to help them make the transition from the class to being an active reproducing member of City Bible Church. Often the teacher is the only pastor many of them have a relationship with, thus it is the teacher's is our responsibility to help them to the next lane of the assimilation freeway. *This is where people often fall through the cracks.*
    2.   Within three or four weeks after the completion of the class, the teacher will personally meet with each class member. In a relational setting, they will discuss the following issues:

a. Answer any questions or concerns about anything taught in the class or answer questions not addressed in the class.
b. Determine if City Bible Church is where they are to become an official member.
c. Determine, in regards to the Healthy Member Profile, where are they, and what areas would they like to take the next step towards. (Water baptism, Spiritual baptism, tithing etc)
d. Define their gifts and callings in regard to serving the Body of Christ, and how they can begin to function in those areas. Facilitate them becoming involved with the appropriate ministries by contacting the appropriate pastor or department head and making them aware of the person who desires to be involved.

III.   CONTENT OF THE MEMBERSHIP CLASS

Chapter One: A People Who Are Planted

Chapter Two: A People With A Vision

Chapter Three: A People With Proper Foundation

Chapter Four: A People Filled With the Spirit

Chapter Five A People Committed to the Church

Chapter Six: A People Committed to the Cell

Chapter Seven: A People Committed to Building Relationship

Chapter Eight: A People Committed to Giving the Tithe

Chapter Nine: A People Committed to Giving A Faith Harvest Offering

Chapter Ten: A People Committed to Prayer

Chapter Eleven: A People Committed to Worship

Chapter Twelve: A People Who Understand Communion

Chapter Thirteen: A People Who Receive Prophetic Ministry

Chapter Fourteen: A People Protected By Church Government

Chapter Fifteen: A People Who Embrace Church Discipline

Chapter Sixteen: A People Who Build Marriage and Family

Chapter Seventeen: A People Who Have Vision For Their City

Chapter Eighteen: A People Who Reap the Harvest of Lost Souls

Chapter Nineteen: A People Who Have a Vision for the World

MEMBERSHIP APPLICATION
9200 NE Fremont, Portland, Oregon 97220

ELDERSHIP & PASTORAL LEADERSHIP:
We as the pastoral leadership of this local church formally receive you this day as a member of our family. We accept this charge before God and this congregation, committing ourselves to your spiritual welfare and protection. By God's grace, we will serve you to the best of our ability.

MEMBERSHIP COMMITMENT:
As a born again Christian, belonging to the church of the Lord Jesus Christ, I publicly identify myself with this local church, accepting the privileges, responsibilities and discipline of a committed member. By God's grace, I pledge myself to be faithful to the vision and values of this church, to be loyal to this church, to serve, and to live according to the standard of the Word of God.

CONGREGATIONAL COMMITMENT:
We the congregation commit ourselves to you as new members of this church. We receive you today into our church family. We will love and serve you and stand with you. We pray God's blessings on you today. May your gifts be released, may God provide for you and may you find many life-long relationships in this congregation. We bless you in Jesus' name.

Signature_____

Vision for a Discipling Church

INTRODUCTION

There was a time in history when craftsmanship was highly esteemed. When items were produced, they were handcrafted originals in which the craftsman had invested his time, energy, creativity, and even something of his own personality. In the early 1900's assembly-line production came into existence. As a result, products which often had taken days, weeks or months to produce were often manufactured in hours. Unfortunately, while the quantity increased, the quality decreased.

We see this crisis reflected in the church today. Many church leaders have given themselves to mass-producing believers. While they claim hundreds or thousands in church attendance, often the quality of the end product has diminished. As Juan Carlos Ortiz once stated, our problem is the eternal childhood of the believer. I suggest that God is interested in the end product (Colossians 1:28-29) and that end product should be a biblical product. The question then arises "What should the end product resemble?" and "Has God given us a biblical pattern to follow?" The crisis at the heart of the church is one of product – the kind of people being produced are inferior to God's standards.

I. DEFINING BIBLICAL PRODUCT

A. Biblical Product in Creation
(Genesis 1:26-28)
1. God created man to a specific standard: His standard. Man was God's product.
2. God's product was character. His purpose was dominion and kingdom rule.

B. Biblical Product in the Old Covenant
1. God's standard of godly character, obedience to God's authority
2. God's desire for a people of prayer and worship
3. God's desire for a people who understand purpose
4. God's willingness to use whatever means necessary to produce a biblical product acceptable to Him

C. Biblical Product in the New Covenant/Gospels
1. To make disciples (Matthew 28:18-20)
2. Willing to deny self, take up their cross and follow Christ (Luke 9:23-25)
3. Puts Christ first before self, family and possessions (Luke 14:25-35)
4. Committed to Christ's teaching (John 8:31)
5. Committed to world evangelism (Matthew 9:36-38)
6. Loves others as Christ loves (John 13:34-35)
7. Abides in Christ (John 15:7-17)

D. Biblical Product as Seen in Acts
1. A person who demonstrates belief by action (Acts 2:37-42)
2. Obedient (Acts 6:7)
3. Paul had disciples (Acts 9:26)
4. Strengthen the disciples (Acts 14:21-24)

E.   Biblical Product as Seen in the Epistles
       (Colossians 1:26-29; Ephesians 4:12-16; Romans 8:29)

F.   Biblical Product Stated

      1.   People who are disciples of Christ and in submission to Jesus as Lord. (Luke 14:25-35; 9:23-25)

      2.   People who are filled with and living by the Holy Spirit. (Ephesians 5:17-18)

      3.   People who are functioning in their spiritual gift(s). (Romans 12:1-6)

      4.   People who are committed to and supporting the local church. (Acts 2:37-47)

      5.   People who are fervent worshippers. (Colossians 3:16; Ephesians 5:17-18)

      6.   People who are faithful prayers (Luke 16:1-10)

      7.   People who are bold sharers of their faith.

      8.   People who are generous givers. (II Corinthians 8-9)

      9.   People who are family builders.

      10.   People who are servants to others.

      11.   People who are overcoming the self-life.

      12.   People who have a world vision.

G.   A.W. Tozer's Seven Marks of a Mature Christian

      1.   A desire to be holy rather than happy.

      2.   A desire to see the honor of God advanced, even if that means personally suffering temporary dishonor or loss.

      3.   A desire to carry your cross.

      4.   Seeing everything from God's viewpoint.

      5.   A desire to die rather than to live wrong.

6. A desire to see others advance at our expense.

7. Habitually makes eternity judgements instead of time judgements.

H. City Bible Church Member Profile
The goal of our ministry to every member is to help them to become a person who is born again, water baptized and filled with the Spirit, who is faithful to the corporate church gatherings, cell ministry and School of Equipping; joyfully gives their tithe & offerings, enjoys prayer, the Word, and worship, has a heart for winning our city to Christ and a vision for world missions, upholds family values and loves God with all their heart, soul, mind and strength.

II. THE PROCESS IN PRODUCING BIBLICAL PRODUCT

A. The Pattern of Processing by Christ

1. Disciple Making was Christ's Approach to a Biblical Product
   a. Jesus made himself available to the multitude but He gave himself to His disciples (Matthew 28:18-20)
   b. Disciple always implies the existence of a personal attachment which shapes the whole life of the disciple, a follower, a student, disciplined one.

2. Discipleship is a matter of personal involvement. (Mark 3:13-15; Matthew 9:35 – 10:5; Luke 6:12; II Timothy 2:2)
   a. It involves personal interest.
   b. It involves personal emotion.
   c. It involves personal appointment.
   d. It involves personal association
   e. It involves personal commission
   f. It involves personal impartation
   g. It involves personal investment

> "It is change not time,
> that turns fools into wise men
> and students into saints."
> A.W. Tozer

B. The Pattern of Processing by the Apostle Paul
1. Paul established local churches. (Acts)
2. Paul established local leadership. (Ephesians 4:12-16)
3. Paul established a product goal. (Colossians 1:26-28)
4. Paul established a process that involved teaching the Word of God, prayer, authority, submission and character development.

C. Practical Suggestions for Processing Toward Biblical Product

1. Do not allow quantity to distort the need for quality.
2. Allow the word of God to set the standard for biblical product, not other churches, trends in culture or accommodating programs.
3. Process toward biblical product by focusing on people individually through small groups, hands-on counseling or discipleship groups.
4. Make apostolic Christianity the pattern. It has been canonized for us.
5. Proclaim the New Testament message of Christ's lordship.
6. Stay sensitive to the ministry of the Holy Spirit in building the church.
7. Establish people in the word of God through a disciplined teaching ministry (include theology, ecclesiology, pneumatology, history and eschatology).
8. Involve the entire church in ministries. Establish a variety of teams to utilize the gifts and calling to meet the practical needs of the church and community.
9. Hold up the historic standard God has given, but also be able to minister to the exception with grace.
10. Provide for the ongoing care of new converts with a view to making them ministers.
11. As people have been trained and are faithful, see that they get new opportunities. And be sure emerging leaders have opportunity to go out and begin new ministries as they are called and approved. (Frustrated would-be-leaders are a major cause of unrest in local churches. It is better to give them a start than reap the unrest.)
12. As the local church expands into translocal outreach, study the role of apostolic ministry. Also explore the effect of your expansion on other churches so that division does not militate against harmonious growth.

DISCIPLESHIP

SHEPHERDING	EQUIPPING	DEVELOPING
1. Care	1. Training for Ministry	1. Training for Personal Growth
2. Immediate Need Focus	2. Task Focus	2. Person Focus
3. Relational	3. Transactional	3. Transformational
4. Service	4. Management	4. Leadership
5. Ministry	5. Ministry by Addition	5. Ministry by Multiplication
6. Immediate	6. Short Term	6. Long Term
7. Feel Better	7. Unleashing	7. Empowering
8. Available	8. Teaching	8. Mentoring
9. Focus on Nature	9. Focus on Specific Ministry	9. Focus on Specific Leader
10. No Curriculum	10. Curriculum Set	10. Curriculum Flexible
11. Need Oriented	11. Skill Oriented	11. Character, Mind/Heart
12. What do they want?	12. What do I need?	12. What do they need?
13. Masses	13. Many	13. Few
14. Maintenance	14. Science	14. Art

© John Maxwell

Vision for a Praying Church

INTRODUCTION

All vision must be birthed in prayer and sustained by prayer. Praying effectively involves the heart and the mouth in positive faith confession. As vision is being shaped by the Holy Spirit, a praying leadership team will allow prayer to be the foundation to accomplishing the vision. The goal of a praying spiritual leader is to motivate the entire congregation into a deeper level of prayer and intercession that would release the supernatural powers of God in an obvious and awesome manner, resulting in awesome harvest.

I.   SEVEN BASIC PRESUPPOSITIONS IN THE THEOLOGY OF INTERCESSION

A.   Intercessory prayer is found in scripture from Genesis to Revelation as a definite kind of prayer God responds to.

B.   Intercessory prayer is modeled by many of God's chosen leaders who practiced the ministry of intercession with awesome results.

C.   Intercessory prayer was a prayer commitment of the first apostles, the first disciples, the first church.

D.   Intercessory prayer was and is the chief ministry of our Lord Jesus Christ, who is the mediator between God and man and is the intercessor for man now.

E.   Intercessory prayer is the responsibility of every church that is ruled by Christ and His word.

F.   Intercessory prayer is being restored to the church world-wide in what might be the greatest unified emphasis since the first church in the Book of Acts.

G.   Intercessory prayer is a call of the Spirit to our church now - today - for the taking of our cities, our region, and our nation for the kingdom of God. A major truth in the Bible

II.   CULTIVATING PRAYER IN EACH INDIVIDUAL BELIEVER
Hosea 10:12 Sow for yourselves righteousness; reap in mercy; break up your fallow ground, for it is time to seek the LORD, till He comes and rains righteousness on you.

- St. Augustine: "O Lord, the house of my soul is narrow. Enlarge it that you may enter in. It is ruinous. O repair it. It displeases your sight. I confess it, I know. But who shall cleanse it? To whom shall I cry out but to you? Cleanse me from my secret faults, O Lord, and spare your servant from strange sins."
- E.M. Bounds: "Inflamed desires, impassioned unwearied insistence delights heaven. Heaven is too busy to listen to half-hearted prayer."

A.   The Preparation of Prayer – "Break up"
Prayer begins with a heart and mind that have been softened and planted with the word of God. "Breaking up" the soil of our heart is a personal commitment to confession and repentance.

B.   The Hindrances of Prayer – "Unplowed ground"
The condition of our heart determines our growth, our fruitfulness and our destiny in God. Even as there are different conditions of soil, there are different heart conditions that must be discerned so we can bring forth great fruitfulness.

C.   The Urgency of Prayer – "For it is time"
We live in the glorious "now" of God. The whole of time is God's arena to work on behalf of and through His faithful ones. He desires that His people be mighty in prayer, experienced in getting prayer answers and undisturbed by the most complex or longstanding needs.

D.   The Focus of Prayer – "To seek the Lord"
It is time to seek the Lord. Seeking prayer is an earnest, continual perseverance birthed from a deep hunger and drive. Seeking prayer is prayer that is Holy Spirit initiated and, through intercession, finds God's will and God's answers.

E.   The Persistence of Prayer – "Until"
Many prayers are granted by God but given up by the ones praying because they stopped praying before the answer came. Without the dynamic of persistence, much prayer remains unanswered.

F.   The Dynamic Presence of Christ in Prayer – "He comes"
Power in prayer comes from the empowering of the Holy Spirit within us. As we use that power in prayer, He continues to empower us for prayer and breathe His Spirit in us.

G.   The Abundant Answers to prayer – "Rains righteousness on you"
The rain of God is symbolic of God's favor, blessings, strength and prosperity. It is prayer that releases the rain of God and allows us to receive the rain of God.

III.   **CULTIVATING PRAYER SPIRIT IN THE CHURCH (Ezekiel 22:30)**

A.   Defining the Words for Intercession

   1.   Hebrew
      a.   Palal (84 times) = To pray, to intervene, mediate as a judge, to come between two parties.
      b.   Paga (44 times) = To encounter, meet with, reach or stretch unto, to entreat, to strike or touch, to attack.

2. Greek
   a. Entunchano = To fall in with, meet with in order to converse, to plead with a person with strong feelings. (Acts 25:24; Romans 11:2; Hebrews 7:25; Romans 8:27,31)
   b. Huperentenchano = To make a petition or intercede on behalf of another. It is used in Romans 8:26-27 or the work of the Holy Spirit in the believer making intercession.
   c. Enteuxis = A lighting upon, meeting with a person by appointment so as to offer petitions, supplications, and prayers on behalf of another. (I Timothy 2:1; 4:5)

B. Ministry of Intercession Defined
   1. "An intercessor is a man or woman or child who fights on behalf of others. As such, intercession is the activity that identifies us most with Christ. To be an intercessor is to be like Jesus because that is what Jesus is like. He ever lives to intercede." (Dick Eastman)
   2. "Intercession can be a part of our lives now, the kind of prayer that works the impossible and sets new boundaries of possibility. The spirit of intercession is a bold understanding through prayer of whatever asserts itself against God's design for mankind. Holy Spirit begotten intercessions forecast new life, new hope and new possibilities for individuals in the impossible." (Jack Hayford)
   3. Intercessory prayer is intensified praying which involves three special ingredients: *identification* of the intercessor with the one whom is interceded for; *agony* to feel the burden, the pain, the suffering, the need; *authority*. This is the gained position of the intercessor, to speak with authority that sees results." (Rees Howells, Intercessor by Norman Grubb)
   4. "It is apparent that prayer lies close to the gift of the Holy Spirit. New Testament prayer was shown variously to be earnest, even importunate, a matter of steadfastness and devotion, a day-by-day continuing of intercession. The church seen in the Book of Acts was given over to the prayer of intercession with supernatural results." (Renewal Theology)

C. Teaching the Congregation on Prayer
   1. *Teach* the whole congregation to respect and use the power of corporate, united prayer.
   2. *Remind* believers of the divine purpose of corporate gathering: to fulfill a divine appointment with God and to experience His presence. Prayer makes this possible.
   3. *Nurture* a conviction and establish a principle that every believer is responsible as a New Testament priest to know how to pray and intercede personally and corporately.
   4. *Understand* the pattern of approach as modeled for us in the Old Testament Tabernacle of Moses.
   5. *Raise up* an interceding church that confronts the powers of hell, releases the true power of God and successfully reaps the harvest.

IV. STRUCTURING TO BE A PRAYING CHURCH

A. Prayer Leadership
1. Prayer priority begins with the overseeing leadership
2. Appointing a prayer pastor

B. Potential prayer ministries in a local church
1. Ministry team intercessors: intercessors who minister during service at altar calls, over water baptism candidates and pray for healing and urgent needs.
2. Service intercessors: prayer covering during the services
3. Third row intercessors: seated behind the pastor during services, they pray for the pastor, the sermon, the visiting ministry, etc.
4. Pre-service soaking prayer: pray for anyone who has a need
5. Event engine room intercessors: pray behind the scenes during special events such as outreaches and conferences
6. Event intercessors: pray for all involved in an event (volunteers, staff, ministers, etc) before, during and after the event
7. City care prayer warriors: pray for prayer requests taken from visitor cards and prayer request cards from members
8. Departmental armor bearers: pray for members of assigned departments
9. Healing prayer: meet in the Prayer Center weekly to pray for the sick
10. Daniel prayer intercessors: pray over the prophetic words spoken over the church
11. Deborah's arise: pray for the prodigals in the church
12. Personal armor bearers: teams formed by each elder and department head to cover them in prayer, meeting with them on a regular basis
13. Prayer guard: prayer covering for specific leaders
14. Three-fold cord intercessors: groups of three who agree to pray together for one another on a consistent basis
15. Downtown intercessors: meet weekly downtown to pray and prayer walk the business and city government districts
16. Operation Clean Up: prayer walking the neighborhoods
17. Prayer center: open 16 hours a day, seven days a week for anyone who wants to come pray

C. Opening Service Intercession
Opening service prayer-intercession is the whole church praying together at the beginning of each corporate church service. This is a strategic kind of praying that prepares the church to enter into the presence of God through Spirit-empowered worship. Prayer-intercession with the whole church seeks to stand in the gap, rebuild spiritual hedges, fill the prayer cup in heaven and reclaim spiritual borders. "All church" prayer intercession has the power to ruin Satan's worst strategies, to destroy his principalities and powers regionally, to bring national revival, to heal the land and to release the supernatural. Surely it must be an integral and vital part of every corporate church gathering.

1. A people in need of prayer

   a. People may come to the corporate service unprepared to hear from God, unprepared to minister to others, unprepared to minister to God.
   b. People may come with busy minds and lives and need time to empty themselves of those things that hinder, letting the spirit take control.
   c. People may come with defeated spirits, family problems, marriage problems, financial problems, moral problems.
   d. People may come with the dust of the world upon them and need a time to spiritually apply the blood of Christ and the water of the Word for cleansing.

2. Kinds of Prayer

   a. Concert prayer: Everyone praying out loud together
   b. Agreement prayer: One pray-er prays and we agree with them
   c. Scripture prayer: Read and pray God's word
   d. Group prayer: Two to four people praying together for a specific request

3. Following the Tabernacle of Moses' Principles of Approach for Opening Service Prayer

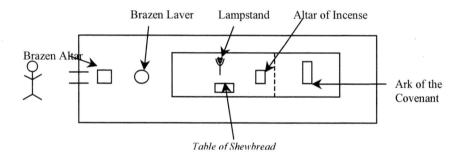

Table of Shewbread

   a. Brazen Altar: Removing guilt through confession of sin and renewing the covenant of grace that guarantees forgiveness and cleansing. (Rev 1:5; 7:14; 22:14; Ez 44:23; I Jn 1:6-9; Jm 4:8)

   b. Brazen Laver: Removing the dust of the world by washing our mind and spirit with the water of God's word, thus judging ourselves. This is a time of taking spiritual inventory and seeing ourselves the way we really are. (Exodus 30:18; Ephesians 5:26; Isaiah 4:4; 6:5; I Peter 4:17; James 1:23-25; I Timothy 2:8; II Corinthians 3:18; Titus 3:5)

   c. Lampstand: Receiving fresh oil of the Holy Spirit and allowing Christ, our High Priest, to trim our wicks and remove all burnt parts so as to release a new powerful flow of His anointing. (Ex 27:21; 30:7-8; Lev 24:3; Eccl 10:1; Mt 25:1-13; Eph 5:18-19; Is 40:31)

d. Table of Shewbread: Receiving our personal, spiritual nourishment by partaking of Christ, the living bread, and of the bread of communion with the saints. In the bread we have life, healing, divine health, spiritual nourishment, and fellowship. (John 6:27-35; 6:48-52; I Corinthians 10:16-21; Matthew 6:11)

e. Altar of Incense: Receiving the power to live as a conqueror by giving our incense before the throne of God in prayer and intercession. (Psalm 141:1-2; 55:17; Rev 8:2-6; Mal 1:11; Ex 30:7-8; Acts 2:42; Lk 1:6-17; 19:46; Ephesians 6:18; Colossians 4:2; Romans 12:12)

f. Ark of the Covenant: Enjoying the presence of God with freedom of spirit, soul and body. Worshipping God with zeal and receiving divine deposits from His presence. His presence is a place of mercy, a place of holiness, reconciliation, communion and the glory of God. (Ex 29:42-46; 30:6; 40:33-38; Num 7:89; Ps 100:4; 22:3; II Sam 6:12-18)

D. Twelve Targets for Opening Service Prayer

1. Pray with supplication. Supplication is a prayer of need and a prayer of request, offering specific petitions. It is a steadfast, continuous, unceasing prayer; an intense spiritual struggle persevering with the petitions.

2. Pray with intercession. To intercede is to mediate, stand in, or identify with. It is to make a petition on behalf of another, to stand in the gap and build a hedge around a person, family, business, church, school, state or nation.

3. Pray with authority. Intercession is an extension of the ministry of Jesus. His authority is now our authority. Our position is one of authority in and through Christ. Pray with confidence. Break bondages, create new hope, and remove spiritual hindrances.

4. Pray against the gates of hell, the powers of the unseen evil underworld. The powers and government of hell will not hold out against the interceding church. The gates of the council of darkness, the plots and destructive strategies can and will be broken down through intercessory prayer.

5. Pray with the keys of spiritual authority. Keys represent the authority the church has to enter certain domains, to bind and loose through intercession. Stop hell's worst, unlock prison doors, shatter Satan's chains, enter the strongman's house and plunder his goods.

6. Pray for the church to be the church as God has meant the church to be: an overcoming, victorious, spiritually powerful church that is fulfilling its first responsibility of intercessory prayer, supplication and gap standing.

7. Pray that in this generation, in this nation and in this city God will find people who will respond to the call of the Spirit to stand in the gap, to turn the tide, to shape history, to strike the winning blow and to build interceding churches that transform cities.

8. Pray for our cities. Stand in the gap for the cities. Believe the power of one person or one church standing in the gap can save a city from hell's destructive powers. Respond with repentance, humility and continuous intercession.

9. Pray for spiritual hedges to be rebuilt. Intercessory prayer invokes the ability to build spiritual walls or hedges around people, houses, marriages, children, businesses, churches, cities and regions. Broken down hedges allow spiritual destruction and demonic attacks.

10. Pray to fill the prayer cup in heaven. Our responsibility is to fill the cup of prayer so that God will pour out from this cup a spirit of mercy and not wrath, of revival not judgement, of healing not destruction. Our prayers are like incense. This necessitates the fire of intensity with intercession.

11. Pray with spiritual travail, a level of intensity marked by a Holy spirit burden to actually bring to pass through prayer a given promise, a prophetic word or a Holy Spirit illuminated need in a person, church, city or nation.

12. Pray with faith to enlarge your spiritual borders or reset your spiritual boundary lines according to God's will. Resist the devil who intends to limit your inheritance and move your boundary lines. Intercessory prayer pushes the boundary lines out according to God's vision and purpose.

V.   OTHER CORPORATE ALL CHURCH PRAYER GATHERINGS

A. Prayer and Praise Sunday: This is when we dedicate the whole service to prayer intermingled with praise.

B. Solemn Assembly: This is when we as a church set aside three days of fasting and prayer together.

C. Paul and Silas Prayer: This is a prayer gathering that has specific target intercession and the church prays until midnight, a four to five hour all-church prayer time.

D. All Night All Church Prayer: This is when we set aside a particular night and prayer from 10:00 p.m. until 6:00 a.m., usually in shifts so the whole night is covered in prayer.

E.   40 Days of Prayer and Fasting: This is when we mark off a 40 day time period, asking the whole church to choose one, two, three or more days a week during the six weeks to fast and pray. We then end this 40 days with a prayer celebration on a Sunday night.

Vision for a Presence of God Church

Repent, therefore, and be converted that your sins may be blotted
out, so that the times of refreshing may come from the presence of
God. Acts 3:19

INTRODUCTION
What is the measuring rod for a successful church? Is it the elegance and size of the building? How about the number of people who attend on Sunday morning or its membership? If you had to rate a church, what criteria would you use to discern its success or its spiritual health.
(Matthew 18:20; Exodus 33:14-16)

"To be in the presence of the Lord is to be revived. When a community of believers is brought low before the presence of the Lord, when the very air that they breathe appears to be supercharged with the sense of His presence – this is the beginning of revival. It is revival!"
J. Edwin Orr, Times of Refreshing

"During a spiritual awakening there is first an overwhelming awareness of the presence of God among His people. I have no hesitation in saying that this awareness of God is the crying need of the church today."
Ted S. Rendall, Fire in the Church

I.   UNDERSTANDING GOD'S PRESENCE

A.   Defining the Word Presence

1.   The Hebrew word paniyam is translated presence 76 times. Paniyam is derived from the root word *pana* which means "to turn the face."

2.   The presence of God in scripture has the idea of God's face being turned toward someone in acceptance and favor. His presence fills up, pervades, permeates, overspreads.

B.   Three Aspects of God's Presence

1. Omnipresence (Psalm 139:6-8; Jeremiah 23:24)

2. Manifested, sovereign presence (Genesis 3:8; 4:16; Leviticus 22:3; II Chronicles 5:11-14)

3. Felt-realized, personal presence (Psalm 22:3; 51:16; 16:11; 31:20; Acts 3:19)

II.   PREPARING TO ENTER GOD'S PRESENCE
(I Peter 2:5-9; Hebrews 9:11-12, 23-24; 10:19-25; Psalm 100:4; Exodus 29:42-46)

A.   The Tabernacle of Moses Model

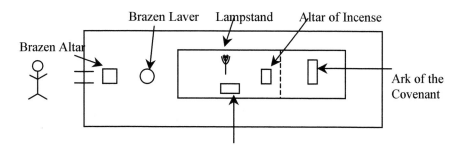

Table of Shewbread

B.   The Priestly Preparation for Entering God's Presence
   1.   Brazen Altar – Blood: Removing guilt through confession of sin and renewing the covenant of grace that guarantees forgiveness and cleansing (I John 1:6-9)
   2.   Brazen Laver – Water: Removing the dust of the world by washing my mind and spirit with the water of God's word thus judging myself. A time of taking personal and spiritual inventory, seeing myself the way I really am.
   3.   Lampstand – Oil: Receiving fresh oil of the Holy Spirit. Allowing Christ, my High Priest, to trim my wick and remove all burnt parts so as to release a new powerful flow of His anointing.
   4.   Table of Shewbread – Bread: Receiving my personal, spiritual nourishment by partaking of Christ, the Living Bread.
   5.   Golden Altar – Incense: Receiving the power to live as a conqueror by offering my incense before the throne of God; prayer and intercession.

III.   ENTERING HIS PRESENCE THROUGH BIBLICAL WORSHIP
Ark of the Covenant: Enjoying the presence of God with freedom of spirit, soul and body. To worship God with zeal and receive divine deposits from His presence. His presence is a place of mercy, holiness, reconciliation, communion, the glory of God. (Psalm 100:4; 22:3)

A.   The Principle of Praise
   1.   We are a royal priesthood (I Peter 2:5-9; Revelation 1:5)
   2.   We are to offer a sacrifice to God (Hebrews 13:15; Psalm 54:6; 116:17; 141:2; 107:22; 27:6)

> *Worship has the power to penetrate hearts, for the childlike beauty and authenticity of it bypasses resistant minds and touches souls with the tender reality of God's presence.*   *Jack Hayford, Majesty*

B. The Recognizable Signs of His Presence
1. Joy and rejoicing (Psalm 16:11)
2. Liberty and transformation (II Corinthians 3:17-18)
3. Refreshing (Acts 3:19)
4. Impossible situations melt (Psalm 97:5)
5. Strength (Isaiah 40:28-31)

IV. A LEADERSHIP COMMITMENT TO BUILD A WORSHIPPING CHURCH

A. Committed to sustaining a fervent worship spirit in our congregation through the biblical expressions of worship as taught in scripture (I Peter 2:5-9).

B. Committed to proper spiritual preparation for worship through opening service prayer for all worshippers, especially those who lead in worship. (Genesis 35:2-3; Exodus 30:18-21; 40:12-16; Hebrews 10:22)

C. Committed to a spirit of excellence in our music (mentioned 839 times in the Bible) and worship ministry, excellence in attitudes, dress, modesty, etcetera.

D. Committed to the river of God as being the power of our worship and the purpose of our worship. I am not interested in techniques, methods and creativity that do not enhance the river of God. All songs and worship should be in the river of God, in the flow of God's Holy Spirit. We are a people of His presence (Acts 3:19).

E. Committed to the teaching of the Tabernacle of David as being the pattern for New Testament worship. (the order of singers and musicians)

F. Committed to the prophetic ministry released in the presence of true worship.

G. Committed to the theology of creativity and spontaneity as it is rooted in God's word, allowing for new, contemporary, cutting-edge expressions in both music and song. God is alive, living, changing and growing through us and our worship must be new, growing, changing and allowing for changes.

H. Committed to worship and praise through instruments as Psalm 150 speaks. We shall endeavor to nurture more skilled musicians, more stringed instruments and more prophetic spirit upon the instruments.

I. Committed to nurturing a dynamic, unified, committed, spirited, anointed, flexible, prophetic, cutting-edge, edifying, stronghold breaking, devil chasing, worshipping church. (I Chronicles 15:16; I Chronicles 20:21; Nehemiah 7:1)

V. THE SCHOOL OF DAVID AND THE WORSHIP DEPARTMENT OF THE CHURCH

A. A School of David where worship, drama and creative ministries can meet for fellowship, relationship building, equipping, ministry expansion and preparation for weekend services.

B. A worship department that builds a variety of music support and expression for the worship services.

C. Acronym for the School of David

Davidic worship
Arts
Voice
Instruments
Drama

VI. SEVEN BIBLICAL BASICS FOR WORSHIP MINISTRY
(I Chronicles 25:1-7; Acts 13:36; Jeremiah 30:21)

A. Dedication: "To be set apart and consecrated for a sacred work"
(I Chronicles 25:1; II Timothy 4:6; I Thessalonians 5:23; Joshua 14:8-9,14; Romans 12:1)
- When Handel composed *The Messiah*, he withdrew for 23 days, hardly eating or sleeping so dedicated was he to this vision in his heart. In *The Hallelujah Chorus* he saw all heaven before him.
- Swiss hermit: "O Lord, take from me what keeps me from Thee. Give me what brings me to Thee. And take myself and give me Thyself."
- Jim Elliot, the Auca Indian martyr, wrote: "God I pray Thee, light those idle sticks of my life that I may burn for Thee. Consume my life, my God, for it is Thine. I seek not a long life, but a full one, like You, Lord Jesus."

B. Prophetic Anointing
(I Chronicles 25:1)

C. Skilled and Disciplined
(I Chronicles 25:1)

D. Servant's Heart
(I Chronicles 25:2)

E.   Teachable and Submissive
      (I Chronicles 25:2-3,6)

F.   House of the Lord Commitment
      (I Chronicles 25:6)

G.   Instructed in the Song of the Lord
      (I Chronicles 25:7)

City Bible Church Qualifications for Worship Ministry Involvement

1. Be a member of City Bible Church: completed the church membership class and been set in before the congregation

2. Be a giver: confirmed by consistent tithing and a spirit of giving in other areas

3. Be a worshipper: using the nine biblical expressions of worship

4. Be a servant: a person who is willing to do whatever is necessary for the whole team

5. Be committed: a person who is faithful in every area of life, work and church. This includes being committed to this department and to the things that make this department successful such as the meetings and services.

6. Be teachable: a person who brings to this department a hunger and thirst to learn the flow and heartbeat and who also has a submissive spirit

7. Be sacrificial: a person who is willing to go over and above normal duties in worship when needed and to give themselves not only to church services but to events, projects and special times when sacrifice is needed

Vision for a Receiving and Releasing Resources Church

INTRODUCTION: Many great visions remain on the drawing board because of the lack of resources. The fuel to move vision from imagination to realization is sufficient resources. These divine and practical resources must be released and channeled into the vision. Resources follow vision. The foundations for financing the vision must be proportionate to the size of the vision being built.

> Vision is that which a congregation perceives by the Holy Spirit as pertaining to God's purpose for them, thereby creating spiritual momentum resulting in spiritual advancement and maintained through spiritual warfare.

I. THE MAN, THE VISION & THE RESOURCES

A. The leaders must pray about, clarify and write the vision.

B. Confirmation of the vision must be birthed in the people.

C. Finances must be gathered for the vision.

D. Believe for a willing spirit in the people

E. Result of obedience and work is that God's glory filled the place.

F. The leader must personally have faith for finances so they can inspire tired and weary people

II. THE FOUNDATION FOR FINANCING THE VISION

A. The Tithe: Cultivating a Proper Perspective
(Deuteronomy 26:1-4)

1. Life in Egypt (Deuteronomy 26:5-7)

2. Deliverance from Egypt (Deuteronomy 26:8)

3. Present blessed position (Deuteronomy 26:9)

B. The Tithe: Cultivating Faith and Obedience
(Deuteronomy 26:10-15)

1. Tithe is the first of our wages and the first of our increase.
2. Tithe is the acknowledgement that all we have belongs to the Lord.
3. Tithe is to be given with an attitude of worship, as a rejoicing offering. (Leviticus 22:17,22,29)
4. Tithe is to be given from our increase also.

5. Tithe is the sacred portion that we set aside as the Lord's. It is holy.
6. Tithe is not to be used for personal needs.
7. Tithe is to be given as an act of spiritual obedience.
8. Tithe is the basis to receive God's covenantal blessings/cursings.
9. Tithe is the provision for the releasing of ministry in the house of the Lord.
10. Tithing is not just Old Testament teaching. Both Jesus and the Apostles confirmed tithing and offerings.
11. Tithing is a biblical minimum and will not limit our giving, but open the door to a genuine stewardship.
12. Tithing is the acknowledgement that God is the owner of all and I am only a steward or trustee over my human estate.
13. Tithing is a token of consecration that one has surrendered all and made Christ Lord.
14. Tithing is the giving of our firstfruits. (II Chronicles 31:5)

C. The Tithe: Cultivating Prayer Warfare Position
1. Standing in prayer believing for the multiple blessings that a tither has rights to.
2. Standing in prayer rebuking the attacks of the devourer.
3. Standing in prayer against the curse the enemy will try to attach to the blessings of God.

III. ENLARGING THE VISION RESOURCES
(Ephesians 3:20; Luke 7:9; Genesis 8:22; I Chronicles 29:14-18)

A. Faith Harvest Giving
A faith harvest offering is given by the believer with the knowledge that this seed is sowed in faith, believing God to water it and enable it to become the full harvest of what God desires to bring into my life. This is a faith offering, a specific giving with liberality and sacrifice.

B. Principles of Faith Harvest
1. A faith harvest offering is given out of a willing heart (Ezra 1:4; 7:16; 96:8; Exodus 25:2; 35:5).
2. A faith harvest offering is given out of a stirring of the Holy Spirit (Exodus 35:21).
3. A faith harvest offering is given out of my own special treasure (I Chronicles 29:3).
4. A faith harvest offering is a sacrificial offering (II Samuel 24:24; Mark 12:41-44; II Corinthians 8:3).
5. A faith harvest offering is motivated by grace not guilt, competition or pressure (II Corinthians 8:1; 9:7-8).
6. A faith harvest offering is a seed faith offering (II Corinthians 9:6).

Vision for a Liberal Giving Church

Cultivating a Giving Spirit that Fulfills Godly Vision
Proverbs 3:9-10

INTRODUCTION

The vision of the leader will be fulfilled in and through the church. The church vision will be enlarged or limited by the amount of resources available. A vision church is a faith church. Faith for finances is one of the building blocks all leaders must know how to lay and how to build upon.

I.   THE GIVING CHURCH GIVER'S PROFILE

A.   Willing Heart
(Exodus 25:2; 35:5,21-22)

B.   Stirred Heart
(Exodus 35:21)

C.   Sacrificial Heart
(Exodus 35:29)

D.   Loyal Heart
(I Chronicles 29:3)

E.   Rejoicing Heart
(I Chronicles 29:9)

II.   THE GIVING CHURCH MODEL PRAYER

I Chronicles 29:10-15 David blessed the Lord before all the assembly; and David said: "Blessed are You, Lord God of Israel, our Father, forever and ever. Yours, O Lord, is the greatness, the power and the glory, the victory and the majesty; for all that is in heaven and in earth is Yours; yours is the kingdom, O Lord, and You are exalted as head over all. Both riches and honor come from You, and You reign over all. In Your hand is power and might; in Your hand it is to make great and to give strength to all. Now therefore, our God, we thank You and praise Your glorious name. But who am I, and who are my people, that we should be able to offer so willingly as this? For all things come from You, and of Your own we have given You. For we are aliens and pilgrims before You, as were all our fathers; our days on earth are as a shadow, and without hope."

A.   We acknowledge His supreme dominion and universal authority.

B.   We acknowledge our total dependence on God

C.   We acknowledge His ownership and our stewardship

D.   We acknowledge our life here as a sojourner

III. THE GIVING CHURCH GROWTH IN GIVING

A. Giving: Giving activates divine law that releases the work of God in our private world.
"Honor the Lord with your substance and with the first fruits of all your increase." (Proverbs 3:9)

B. Receiving: God responds to our giving by opening up opportunities to receive divine provisions both directly and indirectly from His hand.
And your barns will be filled with plenty." (Proverbs 3:10a)

C. Prospering: God desires that we receive abundantly and have more than enough so as to become a liberal giver.
"And your vats will overflow with new wine." (Proverbs 3:10b)

D. Stewardship Lifestyle: A steward is a guardian of the interests of another. The steward owns nothing, but is careful to guard, protect and increase the property of the one whom he serves. We are stewards of time, strength, ability as well as our money.
(Luke 16:1-13)

IV. TWELVE PRINCIPLES IN CULTIVATING A GIVING SPIRIT

A. Giving releases the favor of God upon the giver
(II Corinthians 8:1)

B. Giving, in spite of the affliction of poverty, produces great joy and releases supernatural provision
(II Corinthians 8:2)

C. Giving beyond one's ability, without thought of oneself, breaks the spirit of poverty
(II Corinthians 8:3)

D. Giving in spite of human restraints or human reasoning overcomes smallness of spirit.

E. Giving sacrificially deepens dependence upon God as our only source.

F. Giving should be proportionate to one's spiritual growth in other Christian virtues.

G. Giving that completes commitments which started with inspired faith will establish deep conviction for lifetime giving.

H. Giving is acceptable to God on the basis of the giver's heart, not the giver's amount.

I. Giving allows the Holy Spirit to minister to our deficiency.

J. Giving can be snared by delayed obedience brought about by postponement of generosity.

K. Giving is governed under the laws of harvest
(II Corinthians 9:6)

L. Giving with a joyful attitude pleases the heart of God.

Vision for a Church with Cells

INTRODUCTION

We need a vision to build an enduring church which calls for strong foundational principles and values that are based on the word of God. As the church grows spiritually and numerically, changes will take place. It is the responsibility of the leadership is to process these changes, pace the changes and prepare the different levels of leadership for the changes as well as the congregation. The essence of what makes great churches is their honoring of core values. The context and everything else may change, but core values are not open to change. We value the vision God has given the church, to reach the city and state, nation and nations, by extending God's Kingdom with supernatural power. Establishing a small group ministry is staying with bibilical values, but changing, updating and adapting the methods. The cell is an important part of the future of a church.

I. **SEEKING TO BUILD A NEW TESTAMENT CHURCH**

    A.   New Testament Church Definition
           A local church that is founded upon and patiently moving in and practicing the pattern and principles of New Testament divine order of what the church is to be in all areas. A New Testament Church:
           1.   Has come together to fulfill God's purposes.
           2.   Is structured to a New Testament pattern.
           3.   Is expanding and impacting their neighborhoods, city and region.

    B.   New Testament Church Profile – 15 Essential Marks
           Acts 2-7 describes the first seven years of the church Christ built after His ascension. These chapters describe the Kingdom of God culture in terms of priorities and practices. As we move into our future these are priorities for us as a people of God.
           1.   A Powerful Church, Acts 1:8
           2.   A Witnessing Church, Acts 1:8
           3.   A Prayer Church, Acts 1:14
           4.   A Unified Church, Acts 1:14, 2:1
           5.   A Spirit-Filled Church, Acts 2:1-4, 38
           6.   A Word Church, Acts 2:42
           7.   A Reverent Church, Acts 2:43
           8.   A Sharing Church, Acts 2:26
           9.   A Gathering Together Church, Acts 2:26
           10.   A Supernatural Church, Acts 2:2, 3:1-10, 19:11-12
           11.   A Fellowshipping Church, Acts 2:46
           12.   A Rejoicing Church, Acts 2:46
           13.   A Worshipping Church, Acts 2:46, 15:15-17
           14.   A Likable Church, Acts 2:47-48
           15.   A Growing Expanding Church, Acts 2:42-48

II. THE TWO GROWTH FACTORS OF THE FIRST CHURCH
(Acts 2:41, 47, 4:4, 5:14)

A. Growth Factor #1: The Balanced Heartbeat of the Corporate and the Cell
(Acts 2:46-47)

CORPORATE   **CELL**
Whole Church Gathering   **House to House**
Acts 1:14, 2:1, 41, 44; Hb 10:24-25; 2 Chr 5:11-14   Acts 20:20; Rom 14:7; Heb 3:13 Mt 28:19-20; 1 Jn 3:14-18; Col 1:28-29

B. Growth Factor #2: The Identifying and Releasing of Lay Leadership
(Acts 6:1-7)

III. THE CELL – A MODEL FOR THE FUTURE CHURCH

A. The Cell's Defined Purpose

Connecting people relationally through small groups
(Acts 2:42-47)

Encouraging and equipping every believer to be a disciple of Christ
(Matthew 4:21)

Learning to use homes as a ministry center for reaping the harvest
(Acts 2:46; 5:42)

Loosing people from the powers of darkness through united intercessory prayer
(Luke 4:18-19; Acts 10:38)

Strategic creative ministries to impact the immediate geographical areas
(Matthew 9:35-37; John 4:35-38)

B. The Cell's Balanced Heartbeat
1. Cell Life – Describes the shepherding, pastoral, ministry side of the cell. Caring for and ministering to every member through the cell seven days a week. This is the spirit of community or as Acts 2:42 says, *koinonia*, a partnership, generous sharing.
2. Cell Reach – Describes the harvesting gene within the cell, to be out-reaching not just in-reaching, to apply practically the principles of reaching the city person by person, home by home, neighborhood by neighborhood, thus through the cell seven days a week evangelism will take place.

IV. THE CELL LEADER
(II Timothy 2:2; Matthew 9:35-37, 11:25-30; Luke 14:26-27, 33)

A.   Seven Basic Marks of a Cell Leader
1.   A disciple of Christ.
2.   A shepherd's heart for the people.
3.   A team player with leadership abilities.
4.   An encourager and equipper.
5.   A discipler of others.
6.   A person of prayer.
7.   A person of faith and vision.

B.   Cell Leader Job Description, Requirements and Qualifications
(A sample from City Bible Church)

1.   Job Description
The City Cell leader will help facilitate the vision of the church. They will meet bi-monthly with their group and be responsible for all organizational, planning and shepherding of the flock given to their care. To raise up other potential leaders in the group and to mentor them in leading their own City Cell. Lead the City Cell into making an impact in their neighborhoods in bringing the good news of Jesus Christ through prayer and care evangelism.

2.   Requirements and Qualifications
a.   An official member of our church, regular attendance and an active tither.
b.   Trained in the clear purpose of Cells and their position in carrying out the vision of the church.
c.   Functioning in accordance with I Timothy 5 and Titus 1.
d.   Able to make a two year commitment to leading a cell.
e.   Capable and committed to leading two meetings a month.
f.   Able to lead a meeting, follow approved material, communicate well, and lead discussions.
g.   Facilitate the meetings: keeping order, staying focused, following up needs, visitation, telephone calling, and ministering to the pastoral needs of the group.
h.   Has a vision for evangelism and the ability to equip and inspire the entire group to reach their 'extended congregation' and bring them into a healthy relationship with Christ, His church and His cause.
i.   Works closely with the Evangelism Department and Lay Pastors helping assimilate new people into their City Cell.
j.   Meets with the Lay Pastor in scheduled monthly meetings, keeping them informed of all critical needs in the group.
k.   Be involved in monthly training meetings with Pastor Frank.

Vision for a Networking-Relationship Building Church

INTRODUCTION

The believer is often found in a quest for personal fellowship in an impersonal world. The world is trapped in a maze of alienated lifestyles and life-attitudes. Many in our culture feel the pain of loneliness, uncared for or forgotten. Our society doesn't know it, but they are really wanting New Testament biblical *koinonia*. The norms of culture stress the right to privacy and the primary of non-involvement outside of family membership. Often in church we are trapped by the same norms, not wanting to pry into another's life. As born-again Christians, we are committed to being "knit together" as a spiritual net, networking and growing together. Let us deny the lust of the world that nurtures isolation, alienation and unhealthy independence. Let us all be willing to be tied into the net and, as a net, gather in a great catch of fish. (Matthew 4:18-21; Luke 5:1-10; John 21:1-11; Matthew 13:47)

I.   INSIGHTS FROM THE NET

A.   Defining the Word Net and Network
    1.   Net = a fabric made by interlocking thread by knotting and twisting them at the points where they cross each other. The strength of the net depends on the number of twists or knots made. The net must be pulled and stretched into place.
    2.   Network = a network is held together by secure connections; a network is the total sum of its parts.

B.   Words Describing the Concept of Net
    1.   Knit together (Ephesians 4:16; Col 2:2)
    2.   Joined together (I Corinth 1:10; Eph 2:21)
    3.   Built together (Ephesians 2:22)
    4.   Many members (I Corinthians 12:26)
    5.   One body (I Corinthians 12:12-14)
    6.   Joint supplies (Ephesians 4:16)

II.   TWO ASPECTS OF NETMAKING AND NETWORKING

A.   Leadership Net = the leadership team who have been joined and knitted together by the Holy Spirit into a network of covenantal relationships governed by covenantal commitment.
    (Numbers 11:17,25,29; Proverbs 17:17; Amos 3:3)

B.   Congregational Net = the body of Christ, God's covenant people who are drawn together, twisted, crossed and tied by the Holy Spirit into covenant committed relationships.
    (I Corinthians 1:10; 12:12-31; Ephesians 4:16; 2:21; Colossians 2:2)

III. NET PRINCIPLES

A. The Making of a Net: weaving through building relationships

B. The Washing of a Net: washing through Holy Spirit cleansing and purity

C. The Casting of a Net: willing to get involved with people

D. The Mending of a Net: watchful for relational rippers

IV. THE WEAVING PROCESS – BUILDING AND SUSTAINING RELATIONSHIPS

A. Weaving Begins by Embracing Biblical Concepts of Relationships (Ecclesiastes 4:9-12; Colossians 2:2; I John 4:7; I Peter 3:8; Galatians 6:2; Acts 2:42-46)

B. Weaving Begins by Embracing the Biblical Concept of the Church as Family (Ephesians 1:5; I Peter 2:17; Matthew 12:50; I John 3:1; Ephesians 3:14-15)

C. Weaving Begins by Facing Common Obstacles Hindering Relationships

V. FOUR EXPRESSIONS OF COVENANT RELATIONSHIP
(I Samuel 18:3; Ruth 1:14-18; II Chronicles 23:1; I John 3:16)

A. Covenant Relationship to God—Our Foundation for All Relationships (Jeremiah 31:33; Romans 3:23-25)

B. Covenant Relationship to Our Marriage Partner (Genesis 2:23-24; Ephesians 5:25; Malachi 2:14; Proverbs 2:17)

C. Covenant Relationship to Our Church (Ephesians 5:25-27; Heb 10:25; Ps 26:8)

D. Covenant Relationship to Our Friends (I Samuel 18:1; I Chronicles 12:17; Colossians 2:2,19; Ephesians 4:16; Judges 20:11)
   1. Covenant relationship begins with the act of making covenant (I Samuel 18:3)
   2. Covenant relationship begins with a generous soul attitude (I Samuel 18:4)
   3. Covenant relationship grows as we protect one another (I Samuel 19:1-7)

Vision for an Offense Free Church

Matthew 18:19-20 [Amplified] "If two of you shall agree, harmonize together, make a symphony about anything and everything, whatever they shall ask it will come to pass and be done for them."

INTRODUCTION: The house wisdom builds understands the very essence of evil is fragmentation, division, discord and hatred. The enemy of God's house has a strategy to destroy anything of God's creation that embodies harmony and unity. The attack has been launched against the family (marriage unity), the culture (social unity) and the church — God's house (spiritual unity). For God's people to build a house that resists the spirit of our day, we must build with the pillar of unity. The principle of unity as God's weapon against the kingdom of darkness is revealed from Genesis to Revelation. (Acts 1:14; Acts 2:1; Acts 2:46; Acts 4:24; Acts 4:32; Acts 5:12; Acts 15:25)

I. **THE HOUSE DIVIDED BY UNRESOLVED OFFENSES**
(Matthew 12:25; 24:10)

A. Biblical Definition of Offense
(Mt 5:29-30; 11:6; 13:21,37; 15:12; 17:27; 8:6-9; 26:31,33; Rom 14:21; I Cor 8:13; II Cor 11:29; Rom 14:13; 16:17)

   1. Greek Word — scandalizo, scandalon — meaning: "to spring forward and back, to slam shut, the means whereby one is closed in or trapped, to catch something in a snare, a trap, taking the bait.

   2. Extended Definition
      a. An obstacle on the path over which one falls, stumbles or is hindered
      b. The cause of moral or spiritual ruin
      c. To suffer injury, to come to hurt
      d. To cause a person to begin to distrust, desert one whom before was trusted
      e. To wound with words or actions, violate someone
      f. To act injuriously or unjustly, to be insensitive

B. Signs Detecting Unresolved Offenses
   1. Strained relationships (Proverbs 18:19)
   2. Resist authority (Proverbs 19:20; Hebrews 13:17)
   3. Drifts from and ultimately leaves the local church, their place of planting (Proverbs 17:17; I John 2:19)
   4. Strongholds of vain imaginations (II Corinthians 10:3-4)
   5. Constant satanic harassment (Ephesians 4:27)
   6. River of the Holy Spirit within you and out from you dries up (John 7:37-39)
   7. Bitterness spreads within one's life (Hebrews 12:15)

C.   Resolving Offenses Biblically
(Matthew 18:16-18; 5:23)

1.   The first step toward biblical reconciliation is that every believer accepts the responsibility of taking the initiative in resolving any and all conflicts.
2.   The wisdom of where and when to resolve offenses is needed as well as how to discern which offenses need to be taken to a full two or three party reconciliation. (Colossians 3:13; Ephesians 4:31)
3.   The practicing of biblical forgiveness is necessary in resolving offenses. (Psalm 86:5; 32:1-6; James 5:15; II Corinthians 2:7; Matthew 6:12-15)

II.   ESSENTIAL INGREDIENTS OF BIBLICAL UNITY

A.   United people have the same walk
(Matthew 18:19; Amos 3:3; Ephesians 4:1; I Corinthians 1:10)

B.   United people have a united vision and purpose
(Acts 1:14,21; 2:46; 4:25,32; 5:12)

C.   United People Have A Covenantal Love
(Ecclesiastes 4:9-12; Colossians 2:2; Romans 12:10)

III.   DYNAMIC EFFECTS OF SPIRITUAL UNITY
A.   Success in Spiritual Warfare (Judges 20:11; Isaiah 14:6-7)
B.   The Restoration of Zion's Waste Places (Isaiah 52:8)
C.   The Restoration of Broken Down Walls (Nehemiah 4:16-19)
D.   Answered Prayer (Matthew 18:19; I Peter 3:7)
E.   Continual Supply of the Anointing (Psalm 133; Zechariah 4:6-7)
F.   Fulfilling God-given Visions and Challenges (Genesis 11:5-7)
G.   The House of God Filled With His Glory and Presence (II Chronicles 5:13-14)

IV.   ENDEAVORING TO MAINTAIN UNITY
(Ephesians 4:13)

A.   The Importance of Kingdom Attitudes

B.   The Seven Basic Unity Attitudes
1.   Lowliness
2.   Meekness
3.   Longsuffering
4.   Forbearing
5.   Love
6.   Endeavoring
7.   Peace

Vision for a Lay Ministry Driven Church

I.   **OUR MINISTRY STRATEGY AND LEADERSHIP VISION**

   A.   To see the harvest reaped, assimilated and discipled.

   B.   To structure the church for quality pastoring and regional harvest.

   C.   To train lay people to do the harvesting and pastoring at City Bible Church.

   D.   To be a meta-church. Meta-church indicates both a change of church infrastructure and a change of perspective about how ministry is to be done.

   E.   To become a church with hundreds of lay-led home discipleship centers that multiply remarkably quickly and efficiently.

   F.   To assure the highest level of care at the lowest level in the structure.

   G.   To spread the load to lay pastors, giving the right amount so as not to burn anyone out, but to promote measurable, low-ratio spans of care.

   H.   Our desire is that every person becomes involved with their small group and their small group becomes their church context.

   I.   To limit leaders' scope of responsibility because manageable spans of care enable leaders to provide effective care.

   J.   The goal is to build relationship-based leadership, elevating relationship over programs and methods. Every caring group will build upon relationship as the central focus. Care is birthed out of love and relationship.

   K.   The goal is to mobilize and motivate believers for action and equip them for effective service.

   L.   The goal is for every person to have the availability of a personal pastoral touch through small groups, lay pastors and district pastors.

   M.   The strategy is to establish a structure that pastors the whole church, Cell Group and non-Cell Group people, and facilitates the whole church to cooperate with this plan.

N. To provide a means for people to understand that they are called to the ministry, in the sense that God has gifted them with spiritual gifts which are to be used to serve the Body of Christ.

O. To provide a means for people to understand the concept of what it means to be a minister and to exercise that ministry.

P. To provide a means for people to discover their spiritual giftings by providing teaching on the various gifts and allowing them to take a spiritual gifts questionnaire that will aid them in determining their gifts.

Q. To provide a means for the people to develop their spiritual gifts and to equip the saints to do the work of the ministry.

R. To provide a means for people to deploy their spiritual gifts and get involved in ministry.

II. THE LAY PASTOR AND THE SECOND REFORMATION

We are in the midst of a second reformation. The first reformation put the scriptures into the hands of the laity; this one puts the ministry into the hands of the laity. It is my perspective that lay people, those outside of the ordained ministers, will be the vanguard of the Holy Spirit activity in these days.

The traditional layman's image needs scriptural remodeling. In Switzerland in 1974, Lausanne International Congress on world evangelism had a laymen's night. A panel of business and professional men discussed the role of laymen in the task of world evangelism. The United States representative, a real estate investor, presented an ultimatum to the audience. Laymen would no longer be content with the traditional role assigned to them by religious leaders. Traditionally a good layman was asked to do four things: 1) Regularly attend all church functions; 2) Liberally give money to support church programs; 3) Support all church programs established by the leadership; 4) Adhere to the eleventh commandment, "Thou shalt not rock the boat."

III. LAY LEADERS IN HISTORY

A. The Waldenses. In the 12th century Peter Waldo, a merchant from Lyons, France, wanted to return to the teachings of the New Testament. The scriptures were translated into the vernacular and the laity were encouraged to memorize large portions of scripture. Convinced that laymen could preach the gospel, the movement spread throughout France, Italy, Spain, Germany and Bohemia. The organized church branded the Waldenses as heretics and their numbers were scattered and finally dissipated.

B. John Wycliffe. Wycliffe translated the Latin Vulgate Bible into the language of the people. He taught that laymen could be participators in the ministry, even to the administrating of the sacraments.

IV. LAY PASTOR PROFILE

A. Laity are the people outside a particular profession, as distinguished from those belonging to it, particularly in religious terms. Laity are not members of the clergy.

B. Lay pastor is the recognizing of the pastoral gift in those who are trained and released to do the work of pastoring while still employed full time in secular work.

C. Lay pastor is recognizing the priesthood of all believers. Every believer has both the right and responsibility to be an ambassador for Christ, a significant minister in Christ's work.

D. Kenneth Haughk of Stephen Ministries states, "The priesthood of all believers - lay ministry - drives out all indifference! It develops excitement in the church that multiplies ministry. Congregations that implement a system of intentional training and support of lay ministry become more fully places of love and care, places where the overflowing abundance of God reaches homes, families, and places of work. When the church fails to equip, train and support its members to be the loving, caring community God calls it to be, indifference and apathy become the norm."

V. LAY LEADERS IN SCRIPTURE

A. <u>Daniel</u>. While employed in the political field, Daniel became a force as a spiritual leader to the kings he served. Daniel possessed a prophetic gift that gave direction to the known world of his day.

B. <u>Nehemiah</u>. While employed as a cupbearer, he became a pastor/leader to the people of God. His family background was a prince in Israel, not a priest. As the king's cupbearer, he held a high place of honor in the palace of Shushan and had confidential access to the king. He later became governor of Jerusalem after rebuilding the walls and restoring the people to divine order.

C. <u>Amos</u>. The prophet of judgement, Amos is the author of the minor prophet book that bears his name. He was no professional prophet and does not appear to have belonged to any rank or influence. He did not belong to the order of the prophets, nor had he been educated in the school of the prophets. His profession was that of a dresser of sycamore trees. He was an agriculturist, a farmer. The quiet life of Amos exercised great formative influences upon him. With time to think and pray, he was qualified to form clear judgements. The art of a seer is not cultivated in crowds.

D. <u>Priscilla and Aquilla</u>. The married couple who were tentmakers by trade, became the Apostle Paul's co-partners in the ministry. Paul, also a tentmaker, was attracted to this awesome couple when he went to Corinth and Athens. Paul lived with them for a year and a half while establishing a church. They become strong in discipling, teaching and hospitality.

E. Onesiphorus. He was a lay leader in Ephesus who befriended the Apostle Paul (II Timothy 1:6; 4:19). He was probably an elder in the church at Ephesus. This man opened his house to be used as a center of spiritual activity. A man with the deep compassion of a pastor's heart, he ministered to Paul while Paul was in a deep trial.

F. Epaphroditus. Epaphroditus was a lay leader who possessed a commendable character and a wonderful pastor's heart (Philippians 2:25; 4:18). He was a companion in labor, a fellow soldier and a man who laid his life on the line for the opportunity show love and encouragement to others. He was a remarkable person of compassion.

G. Lydia. Lydia was a very successful business woman in a very prosperous city (Acts 16:12-15,40; Philippians 1:9-10). Thyatira, her home city, had many guilds. One was that of "dyers." The water of the area was so well adapted for dying that no other place could produce the scarlet cloth like Thyatira. This unique purple dye brought the city universal renown. Lydia was a well-known, very successful seller of this product. She became Paul's first convert and was the beginning of the Philippian church.

Vision for an Equipping Church

> "And He Himself gave some to be apostles, some prophets, some evangelists, and some pastors and teachers, for the equipping of the saints for the work of ministry, for the edifying of the body of Christ, till we all come to the unity of the faith and of the knowledge of the Son of God, to a perfect man, to the measure of the stature of the fullness of Christ."
>
> Ephesians 4:11-13

I.   THE LEADERSHIP CALL IS TO BE EQUIPPERS

A.   Defining the Word "Equip":

1.   Greek - [*Katartismos*] - Preparing or training, to complete thoroughly, to repair, to adjust, a craftsman.

2.   *Katartismos* translated:

a.   Mending

"Going on from there, He saw two other brothers, James the son of Zebedee, and John his brother, in the boat with Zebedee their father, mending their nets..." (Matthew 4:21).

James and John were bringing the broken strands of their nets together with the other strands so as to make their net function properly. They were mending, adjusting and equipping the net to do the work of fishing. Those strands that had been broken under the pressure of their work had to be mended. What they were doing in the natural was prophetic of what they were destined to do in the spiritual, to mend the church, for Jesus had called them to be "fishers of men."

Mending the lives which are broken is the work of the governmental ministries to the body of Christ. The governmental ministries are to bring those strands that have been broken and battered together with other strands so as to make a strong net which will do the work of catching fish (or souls) for Jesus. When the net broke, James and John did not dive into the water and try to do the work of the net in catching the fish. They were, rather, restoring that part which was broken so that the net itself could function in its work. There are many pastors in the church today who try to do the work of the whole body instead of fulfilling their ministry of equipping the body to do the work.

b.   Fitted

"The vessels of wrath fitted to destruction." (Romans 9:22).

Here the Greek word is used to describe the fitting or forming of clay into vessels by a potter. God is the potter who is making vessels of honor or vessels of wrath. A person can respond to the Lord in having his life as pliable clay, or, he can reject the hand of God's shapings. The Lord is the source of all adjustments and corrections. The governmental ministries are His hand to be instruments which the Lord uses to bring that correction.

c.   Perfectly Joined Together

"Now I plead with you, brethren... that there be no divisions among you, but that you be perfectly joined together in the same mind and in the same judgment." (I Corinthians 1:10)

The Corinthian church had been torn from within by the spirit of schism and division. The Apostle Paul's desire was for the church to have all the joints and parts of the body which were out of place to come into adjustment. Paul wanted a mending to take place in the body so that it could function with complete coordination. There is a great need in the church for the five-fold ministries to be released to their proper function of healing wounds and building again that which has been broken down. The only way that the body of Christ will ever be perfectly joined together will be when these ministries are able to fulfill this work in the body.

d.   Prepared

"Therefore, when He came into the world, He said: 'Sacrifice and offering You did not desire, but a body You have prepared for Me.'" (Hebrews 10:5).

The passage quotes a Messianic prophecy found in Psalms 46:6. The body "prepared" for Jesus was a human body of flesh and bones, prepared by the Holy Spirit in Mary's womb. When Jesus came into the world, he came into a "prepared" body for the single purpose of doing the Father's will. As a sinless and perfect body was prepared for the Lord Jesus, so God is preparing a many-membered body through which His Son is continuing His spiritual ministry on the earth. The Father is using the governmental ministries to prepare and perfect the body (the church) so that it can accomplish His eternal purpose of subjugating all things under the feet of Jesus Christ.

e.   Framed

By faith we understand that the worlds were framed by the word of God (Hb 11:3)

Here the writer is not talking about the original act of the creating of the worlds, but rather the putting in order, arranging and fitting for use of that which was already existent. The already created worlds were set in order by the Word of God. The universe was adjusted or arranged by God's Word. Similarly, the power of the spoken Word of God will be seen through the governmental ministries as they help to bring the body of Christ together.

3. Classical Greek usages of *Katartismos*
   a. Setting in order a city which had been torn apart by factions and schisms.
   b. The outfitting or preparing of a ship for a long journey.
   c. The preparing of an army for the purpose of battle.

B. Word Pictures to Describe Equippers
1. Trainers of the soldiers in the army of the Lord
2. Restorers of the broken bones of the body of Christ
3. Framers of the boards of God's House
4. Exercisers of the muscles in Christ's body
5. Shapers of the stones in the Temple of the Lord
6. Healers of the breaches in the hedge of God's garden
7. Liberators of those who are bound
8. Adjusters of those who are out of joint
9. Menders of those who are torn
10. Equippers of the body of Christ
11. Placers of God's people
12. Organizers of the Lord's Kingdom
13. Molders of God's clay vessels
14. Seers for God's service

II. THE LEADERSHIP OBSTACLES TO EQUIPPING

A. The Obstacle of Faulty Concepts and Perspective of Pastors and Leaders

B. The Obstacle of Character and Emotions of Pastors and Leaders

C. The Obstacle of Wrong Attitude Toward Lay-People
1. David Watson: "Most Protestant denominations have been as priest-ridden as the Roman Catholics. It is the minister, vicar or pastor who has dominated the whole proceedings. In other words, the clergy-laity divisions have continued in much the same way as in pre-Reformation times, and the doctrine of spiritual gifts and body ministry have been largely ignored."
2. John Stott: "Laity is often a synonym for amateur as opposed to professional, or unqualified as compared to expert."
3. The church is fundamentally a charismatic community for the *charismata* (grace gifts) have been distributed to all. This makes each person an initiating center for ministry.
4. Lay-Person - this is a scriptural word filled with dignity and honor, *laos* portrays a sense of specialness.
   • *Deuteronomy 7:6 "For you are a holy people [laos] to the Lord your God; the LORD your God has chosen you to be a people [laos] for Himself, a special treasure above all the peoples on the face of the earth."*
   • *Leviticus 26:12 "I will walk among you and be your God, and you shall be My people."*

- *I Peter 2:9 "But you are a chosen generation, a royal priesthood, a holy nation, His own special people, that you may proclaim the praises of Him who called you out of darkness into His marvelous light."*
- *Titus 2:14 "Who gave Himself for us, that He might redeem us from every lawless deed and purify for Himself His own special people, zealous for good works."*

5. A layperson, *laos*, is nothing less than a new humanity, the vanguard of the future, the prototype of the Kingdom of God not yet completed. A person of the future living in the present. Next time we hear someone say, "I'm just a layperson," say, "That's more than enough!"

III. EQUIPPING SAINTS - SPIRITUAL AND PRACTICAL APPLICATION

A. Ministry Focus of Mending and Restoring
1. To fix what is broken. Something is broken when it cannot perform the function for which it has been designed, when it is disjointed or disconnected it must be restored.
2. Our ministry attitude must first be:
    - We take you as you are. Grace is dispensed here.
    - We pay attention to brokenness in lives of people. We mend, we pray, we counsel, we bring healing.
    - We're a restoring church. We restore people back to proper working order.

B. Ministry Focus of Preparing and Training
1. This can only take place after the individual has been properly healed, restored, fixed, and brought to a level of maturity that can handle the disciplines of being discipled for taking responsibility.
2. We must allow people to discover their capacity, aptitudes and abilities for the work of ministry and then help them refine their skills.
3. We must help people discover their spiritual gifts and allow them to develop and dispense these gifts. We are a training center. We should desire to motivate and fan the flames of desire in people to discover and use their spiritual gifts.
    a. Usages of spiritual gift tests
    b. Methods of training for lay people: night schools, Saturday schools

C. Ministry Focus of Releasing and Encouraging
1. The Ephesians 4:12 passage clearly states that the saints should <u>do</u>, not just <u>know</u>, the ministry. We must make room for all people to take the burden of ministry in the body and out from the body.
2. The eldership, a pastoral ministry, must take the attitude of encouraging people as they develop their ministry gifts.
    - Modeling - I do it.
    - Mentoring - I do it and they are with me.
    - Monitoring - They do it and I am with them.
    - Multiplying - They do it and I am in the background.
    - Equipped - They do it!

IV. AN EQUIPPING CHURCH MODEL: THE SCHOOL OF EQUIPPING

A. Purpose of the School of Equipping
The School of Equipping is a systematic teaching program created to equip every believer "for the work of ministry (Ephesians 4:12)." The School will consist of eight teaching tracks: Church life, Family Life, Personal Growth, Bible Truths, Pastoral Development, Youth Issues, Prayer Intercession and Intercultural Ministries. Each quarter these eight tracks will offer a different selection of classes to choose between.

B. Structure of the School of Equipping
There are four types of classes offered for each track.

1. *The 100 Series* are foundational classes, those necessary for a strong Christian life. These are essential for every believer, both new and old. For the new Christian, they provide a strong foundation on which to build a new life in Christ. For those who have been serving the Lord for a long time, these are excellent refresher classes to remind us of the foundations we built our lives on and to strengthen those foundations.

2. *The 200 Series* are developmental classes. These classes are designed to develop our spiritual muscles that we might be better prepared both to do spiritual warfare in our own lives and those around us as well as to be effective ministers of the gospel to those in our workplace, our neighborhoods and our families.

3. *The 300 Series* are electives. Is there an area that you would like to learn more about? An area of particular interest to you? Find an elective in that area and expand your horizons. If you are interested in an area that is not listed, then write down your idea and give it to the team leader for that track.

4. *The 400 Series* are leadership development. These classes are designed for those who are in or who desire to be in a specific area of ministry in the church with the exception of the Pastoral Development track which is all leadership training.

C. School of Equipping Schedule

1. *Weekly Format*: The first and third Sundays of each month we have our normal evening service with prayer, worship and normal church activity such as baby dedications, sending and receiving our missionaries, etc. The equipping tracks begin after worship at 6:45 except for the Pastoral Development classes which begin at 6:00.

2. *Term Format*: The School has eight tracks running simultaneously with selections from each track offered each quarter. There will be three quarters: fall, winter and spring. Each quarter will consist of five Sunday evenings and will run during the following times:
    * Fall Quarter: September through November (no classes in December)
    * Winter Quarter: January through March
    * Spring Quarter: April through June (no classes in July and August)

D.   Children's Program
1.   *Nurseries*: Nurseries are provided for children through two years of age. They open at the beginning of every service.
2.   *Preschool Classes*: Preschool is for children ages two through five. Preschool classes begin at the same time that the adults are dismissed for their classes and use the Gospel Light curriculum. This curriculum instills solid biblical foundations important in forming Christian values in children's lives.
3.   *Elementary Children*: All elementary age children meet together in the Ivy Hall for a fast-paced, fun-filled evening. This ministry time includes games, music, prizes and teaching using the well-proven Kids' Church curriculum provided by Metro Ministries from New York City.

E.   Track Descriptions
1.   *Church Life:* This track offers classes in the area of building relationships, worship principles and power, church membership, prophetic gifts and ministry, harvest ministries, evangelism and apologetics.
2.   *Family Life:* This track will offer classes on family, marriage, parenting, single living, blended family, finances in the home, culture pressure, recovering from family breakdown.
3.   *Bible Truths:* This track introduces you to the Bible, first offering an overview of the Bible with Bible survey classes then focusing on a number of different books of the Bible. Basic doctrine and how to read and study your Bible will also be taught.
4.   *Prayer Intercession:* This track will cover everything from basic devotional prayer to principles of intercession, informed intercession, prayer in the home, prayer in the neighborhood and the marketplace, principles of deliverance, healing and spiritual warfare.
5.   *Personal Growth:* This track will offer teaching on how to grow in Christ, break bad habits and gain spiritual freedom, live by principles, walk in newness of life, character development, and decision making. Special areas also included are business success and personal financial success.
6.   *Youth Issues:* The youth will have three age-distinctive levels functioning at the same time: junior high, high school and college age. The issues covered will be wise foundations, wisdom versus foolishness, convictions, how to pray, principled living, moral purity, right music choices, handling conflicts, building godly friendships and living with standards.
7.   *Pastoral Development:* This track is designed to raise up, train and equip the lay person to pastor the flock and would include classes such as cell leaders training, lay pastors training, lay counselors training, etc. It also includes church planting classes for those being sent out to plant churches.
8.   *Intercultural Ministries:* Become a "world" Christian, one who has Christ's heart for the nations. This track focuses on the world-wide global vision of Christ for His church. Covering both local and international cultural ministries, this track addresses the issues of world missions as well as ministering to different ethnic groups in our own city.

Vision for a Leadership Developing Church

INTRODUCTION: The church of today needs qualified leadership to lead her to the victories of tomorrow. Where does a pastor find the qualified leader? Should the pastor raise up his own or import them from a college or another like-natured church? If the pastor does choose to train his own, what methods are to be used? What qualifications should the leader possess? The Bible is the source book for all pastors who are endeavoring to build a healthy local church. Concepts and principles of raising up local leaders should be established upon biblical premise. In this study we will cover the following areas:

Philippians 2:20　　For I have no man likeminded
　　　　　　　　　　...or equal soul
　　　　　　　　　　...as interested as I am
　　　　　　　　　　...for I have no one else as near of my own attitude
　　　　　　　　　　...for I have no one else of kindred spirit
　　　　　　　　　　...no one like disposed

　　　　　　　　　　Likeminded: isopsychos (from *isos* meaning equal and *psyche* meaning soul)
　　　　　　　　　　…Equal in soul
　　　　　　　　　　…Of like soul or mind
　　　　　　　　　　…Kindred spirit

I.　GATHERING POTENTIAL LEADERS – THE NECESSARY RISK

　　A.　The Risk of Gathering Imposter Leaders
　　　　(Acts 28:3; Isaiah 11:1-3)

　　B.　The Risk of Gathering Untested Leaders
　　　　(Mt 8:18-27; Jn 6:1-20; Lev 1:7-17; Mt 3:11-12; I Cor 3:13; I Peter 1:7; Rev 3:18)

　　C.　The Risk of Gathering Unstable/Unfaithful Leaders
　　　　(James 1:8)

　　D.　The Risk of Gathering Disloyal Leaders

　　E.　The Risk of Gathering Contentious Leaders

　　F.　The Risk of Gathering Whirlwind Leaders

II.　GATHERING POTENTIAL LEADERS –　THE DIFFERENT BACKGROUNDS

　　A.　Team Leadership: Team leadership are the people that have gone out with a pastor to establish a local church. These people for the most part are stable, loyal and specifically marked people. Nevertheless, they too must be birthed into the pastor's ministry.

B.   **Inherited Leadership**: This type of leadership comes with the already existing church taken over by a new pastor. Sometimes they are qualified good leaders and sometimes they have great need. They have already been doing certain tasks and have formed certain concepts of the local church.

C.   **Transplanted Leadership**: This type may come from a variety of different situations – Bible college, denominational church, another restoration-type church, family, etc. In the natural when a doctor transplants a heart, liver, kidney or any vital organ, it takes considerable carefulness and mature wisdom. Even after such precaution, the body may turn on the foreign part and destroy the proper functioning of the whole body.

D.   **Traditional Leadership**: This type of leadership is the kind that the pastor at first feels very safe in using or in training. They may have excellent character qualities and be very sincere in their willingness to work with the pastor. The problem many times is their <u>root</u> ideas, concepts, vision, etc. If the pastor begins to use them before he knows their roots, he will have great difficulty in protecting the local body.

E.   **Novice Leadership**: This type may be well equipped in fundamental knowledge and necessary character, but when in the actual pressure and demands of the ministry many novices have been destroyed by the presumption and lack of wisdom of the pastor in using them too soon. God will not entrust spiritual authority and leadership to those who have not been tested. Leadership is given to those who are not likely to be blinded by pride or jealousy, whose consecration has been tested and proved, those with the touch of experience. (I Timothy 3:1-9; Titus 1:5-9; I Peter 5:1-9)

F.   **Home Grown Leadership**: This type of leadership have been sowed or planted in the local church at an early spiritual age. They have been filled with the ingredients that make up that particular local church and have been discipled and equipped.

III.   BIRTHING KINDRED LEADERS
(Genesis 14:3; Psalm 87:1-7)

A.   Birthed into the Main Elements of the Local Church
(Proverbs 29:18; II Chronicles 4:20; I Chronicles 15:13)

   1.   The Vision of the House

   2.   The Principles of the House

   3.   The Philosophy of the House

   4.   The Standards of the House

   5.   The Doctrines of the House

   6.   The Procedures of the House

   7.   The Spirit of the House

B. The Birthing Process
1. Spiritual identification with the local church
2. Spiritual illumination of the inner man
3. Spiritual inquiry with the local church
4. Spiritual inspiration to others
5. Spiritual integrity that is proven in the storm
6. Spiritual intensity evidenced in faithfulness

IV. IDENTIFYING POTENTIAL KINDRED LEADERS

A. Positive Identification Marks
(I Timothy 1:12; II Timothy 2:2; Luke 6:1-12)

1. Faithfulness in all areas
2. Humility when corrected or adjusted
3. Willingness to serve in menial areas
4. High level of personal integrity
5. Responsiveness to preaching and teaching
6. Genuine love for people
7. Sensitivity to the needs of others
8. Continual personal growth
9. Successful relationships on the personal, family and occupational level
10. Strong hunger for the Lord and the Word of God

B. Negative Identification Marks
1. Inability to keep confidences
2. Hasty in decision making
3. Constant poor judgements (even after instruction)
4. Aggressive and domineering in relationships
5. Emotional instability
6. Pushing for promotion and recognition
7. Constantly on the wrong side of decisions
8. Continual conflicts with those under their charge
9. Continual justifying and blameshifting

V. TIMOTHY TRAINING – A MODEL FOR LOCAL CHURCH LEADERSHIP DEVELOPMENT

A. The Timothy Training Program is a step by step training program for those who have already shown signs of leadership potential and can be done in either a small group setting or in a classroom setting. Times of teaching are combined with discussion of the practical application of the teaching.

B. Lessons in the Timothy Training Program

1. Introduction to the Life of Timothy: The Invitation

2. Life of Timothy: The Response
   a. Heart conditions
   b. Personal obstacles

3. Local Church Proving and Preparation I
   a. Planting
   b. Discipling
   c. The proving process

4. Local Church Proving and Preparation II
   a. Faithfulness
   b. The importance of the proving process

5. The Choosing I: The Selection
   a. The doctrine of election
   b. Confirmations to God's choosing

6. The Choosing II: The Character Factor
   a. Character qualities from Timothy
   b. Character qualities from Titus

7. The Equipping
   a. The relational foundation for equipping and ministry experiences
   b. The difference between impartation and information
   c. Nine things Timothy received from Paul

8. Placement
   a. Pastoral charges to Timothy
   b. Personal application of these pastoral charges

9. Promotion
   a. God's delays in promotion
   b. Wrong concepts of promotion

10. Progress and Perseverance
    a. Threats to perseverance
    b. Value of perseverance

11. Perspective
    a. The demand for sacrifice
    b. The leader's secret of success

Vision for Restoring and Rebuilding Spiritually Whole People

SEVEN STEPS TOWARD SPIRITUAL HEALTH, FREEDOM AND MATURITY

Introduction: The church of today must be ready for the modern day harvest that will be reaped. Today's unsaved person is unlike people of the past generations. We are a post-Christian, post-modern generation reaping the consequences of a fragmented society, family breakdown, moral confusion, rampant immorality of every kind, occultism, new age mixed with eastern religions. We are a nation that basically denies the Bible and the God of the Bible. When people come to Christ they come broken, wounded, unstable, spiritually bankrupt and emotionally frazzled. The journey from salvation to maturity is something long and uncharted for most who start this new transformation. The church today must have a vision to process people into spiritual wholeness, healing and spiritual health.

I.   **Spiritual health, freedom and maturity begins with a clear understanding of our position in Christ.**

      A.   Our Position in Adam: Fallen
             (Romans 5:12,18-19)
             1.   A nature that is tainted and self-centered (Matthew 7:21-23)
             2.   Slave to sin (John 8:34)
             3.   Born into sin and shaped by sin
             4.   Without excuse (Romans 3:9,19-20)

      B.   Our Position in Christ: Redeemed
             (Romans 5:10-11,17-21)
             1.   Forgiveness of sins (Matthew 26:28; Ephesians 1:7; Hebrews 9:22; John 5:24)
             2.   Child of God (John 1:12)
             3.   Slave of righteousness (Romans 6:18)
             4.   Joint her with Christ (Romans 8:17)
             5.   Dwelling place of God (I Corinthians 3:16; 6:19)
             6.   New creation (II Corinthians 5:17)
             7.   God's workmanship (Ephesians 2:10)
             8.   Hidden with Christ in God (Colossians 3:3)
             9.   Filled with light and not darkness (I Thessalonians 5:5)
             10.   An enemy of the devil (I Peter 5:8)
             11.   Born of God (I John 5:18)
             12.   Set apart with a God-given destiny (II Timothy 1:9; Titus 3:5)
             13.   Seated by the power of the Holy Spirit (Ephesians 1:13-14)

II.   **Spiritual health, freedom and maturity is achieved as the believer overcomes that evil spiritual capacity within called the flesh.**

A.   Flesh is the seat of sin in man
(Romans 8:3-4; Galatians 5:16-19).

B.   The believer's sanctification
1.   We have been sanctified (Hebrews 10:10,14; 13:12).
2.   We are sanctified now (Romans 6:22; I Corinth 1:30; Hb 10:10).
3.   We are being sanctified continually (I Peter 1:15-16).

C.   The power of the sin nature
1.   Functions in the realm of rebellion against the law of God (Rom 7:21-25)
2.   Seeks to forbid the practice of spiritual good in the life of the believer (Romans 7:14-20)
3.   Is capable of all sort of evil (Galatians 5:19-21)
4.   Can be used by the devil as a tool to gain control in the believer's life (Ephesians 4:27)

D.   The believer's responsibility to conquer the sin nature
1.   Decide to separate from sinful influences (II Corinthians 6:17)
2.   Decide to cleanse ourselves from all defilement (II Corinth 7:1)
3.   Decide to rededicate ourselves to God and resist being conformed to the world (Romans 12:1-2; John 2:15-16)
4.   Decide to lay aside every sin that hinders us (Heb 12:1)
5.   Decide to take every thought captive (II Corinthians 10:5; 11:3)
6.   Decide to crucify the flesh with its passions and desires (Gal 5:24)
7.   Decide to shun youthful passions (II Timothy 2:21-22)
8.   Decide to deny ungodliness and live sensibly, righteously and godly in this present age (Titus 2:11-12)
9.   Decide not to yield your members to unrighteousness (Rom 6:13)

III.   **Spiritual health, freedom and maturity is achieved as the believer cultivates and guards a healthy spirit.**

A.   The components of the redeemed spirit
1.   Intuition: to know things by the revelation of the Holy Spirit (Mark 2:8; 8:12; Luke 1:47)
2.   Communion: Power to interact with God (John 4:24)
3.   Conscience: reproving sin and approving what is right

B.   Descriptions of a healthy spirit
      (I Corinthians 2:9-16; 3:1-3)

C.   Warning signs of an unhealthy conscience
      (Gen 3:1-11; Prov 21:2; 14:14; 15:12; Rom 2:1-3; I Sam 15:22; Psalm 32:1-4)

D.   Description of a healthy conscience
      (Acts 23:1; I Tim 1:5,19; 3:9; Hebrews 9:14; 13:18; Acts 24:16; II Tim 1:3)

E.   Removing a common conscience virus: an unforgiving spirit
      (Psalm 51:1; Hebrews 9:14; 10:22; I John 1:9; Genesis 50:19-21; Luke 23:34)

IV.   **Spiritual health, freedom and maturity is achieved as the believer purifies and strengthens the three divisions of the soul: the mind, the will and the emotions.**

A.   The soul
      1.   The soul is the principle of life; the source of emotions, mind, thoughts, reasoning, volition, desires and decisions; the seat of personality.
      2.   The confessions of a struggling soul (Romans 7:14-25)
      3.   The soul's faith position (Galatians 2:20; Romans 6:6)
            a. Believes more than it experiences
            b. Believes sin's power has been cancelled
            c. Refuses obedience to sin's enticements (Romans 6:11-12)
            d. Makes a critical resolve (Romans 6:13-14)

B.   The mind
      1.   The mind is the seat of thinking and reasoning, thoughts and intents (II Corinthians 10:3-5).
      2.   The unhealthy mind is uncontrolled, unguarded and tormented, full of evil thoughts (Romans 1:28; I John 4:18; Genesis 6:5; Jeremiah 4:14; Matthew 15:19; Mark 7:21).
      3.   The healthy mind is a controlled, guarded and transformed mind (Romans 12:3; Ephesians 4:23; Isaiah 55:7-9; II Corinthians 5:13).
      4.   Build and sustain a healthy mind through the disciplines of meditating on and memorizing God's word (Ps 37:31; Col 3:16).

C.   The will
      1.   The will is the ability to choose, determine and carry out plans. A man's will is his organ for decision making.
      2.   Changes of a will in decline

D.   The emotions

1.   Five facts about emotions
   a.   They can be ruled or controlled (Proverbs 25:28).
   b.   They can be changed (Psalm 42:11).
   c.   They can be aligned (II Corinthians 5:7).
   d.   They can be focused (Matthew 22:37).
   e.   They can be Holy Spirit empowered (Galatians 5:22).

2.   Transforming our emotional world
   a.   Emotional world before the cross: fear, despair, anger, resentment, bitterness, inferiority, guilt.
   b.   Emotional world brought under the cross: repentance and regeneration
   c.   Emotional world transformed by salvation and the continued work of the Holy Spirit: using our emotions to love God, focus on the things of God and minister to people.

V.   **Spiritual health, freedom and maturity is achieved as the believer aligns his total life under God's authority and all delegated authority**
(Matthew 8:5-10)

A.   Restoring authority structures in our lives
   1.   Aligning our life under God's authority (James 4:7; Psalm 7:1; 119:2)
   2.   Aligning our life under the authority of God's word (Hebrews 4:12; Psalm 119:18; 138:2; Matthew 4:4)
   3.   Aligning our life under the authority of the home (I Corinthians 11:3; Colossians 3:20; Ephesians 6:1; 5:22)
   4.   Aligning our life under the authority of God-appointed leadership in the local church (Matthew 16:16-18; Titus 2:15; I Peter 5:5; II Corinthians 10:8)
   5.   Aligning our life under the civil authority of our land (Daniel 2:37-38; 4:17; Romans 13:1)

B.   Removing rebellion that destroys authority structures
   1.   Removing rebellion by restoring our place under God's authority structure through coming under (Genesis 16:9; Judges 9:29)
   2.   Removing rebellion by restoring our place under God's authority through obedience and submission (John 14:15; 15:10)
   3.   Removing rebellion by restoring our place under God's authority will restore our spiritual authority (Lk 9:1; 7:7-8)

VI. **Spiritual health, freedom and maturity is achieved as the believer develops a life in the Holy Spirit that results in personal life power, transformation and release of spiritual gifts**
(John 7:37-39; Matthew 20:20-28)

    A.   Receiving the Baptism of the Holy Spirit
        1.   Acts 2:39; Isaiah 44:3,19; John 7:37-38; Ephesians 5:18
        2.   To be filled with the Holy Spirit is to experience Christ as he unselfishly shares with us the same power for living and serving that he experienced himself, the power of the Holy Spirit (Acts 2:4; 8:14-17; 10:44-46; 19:1-6).
        3.   The believer's prayer language (I Corinthians 14:2,4,14,; Romans 8:26-30; Galatians 4:6; Romans 8:15).

    B.   Receiving the Power of the Holy Spirit
        (Acts 1:8; 2:22; 8:13; 19:11; I Cor 12:10; 4:20; II Tim 1:7; Isaiah 11:3; 40:26-29; Col 1:9-11; Eph 3:14-16)

    C.   Receiving the Gifts of the Holy Spirit
        (I Corinthians 12:1-10; Romans 12:1-9; II Peter 3:15)

VII. **Spiritual health, freedom and maturity is achieved as the believer matures in spiritual warfare, learning to use spiritual weapons and wear spiritual armor**
(Ephesians 6:10-17; Luke 11:20-23; Romans 13:12; II Corinthians 6:7)

    A.   The Believer's Spiritual Armor
        (Ephesians 6:10-17)
        1.   Belt of truth
        2.   Breastplate of righteousness
        3.   Shoes of peace
        4.   Shield of faith
        5.   Helmet of salvation
        6.   Sword of the Spirit

    B.   The Believer and Spiritual Warfare
        1.   The invisible realm of Satan's kingdom
        2.   The demonic evil spirits that believers may encounter
        3.   The biblical view of deliverance for believers

ALL THINGS NEW MODEL

"All Things New" is designed to provide a biblical foundation to assist all levels of believers. The focus is for the believer to gain new liberty in their Christian walk by breaking off hindrances and old habit patterns that have resisted personal growth and maturity.

I. Section #1: The Cross
    A. The Life and Purpose of Jesus
    B. The Story of Your Life – The Cross Applied
    C. Old Nature
    D. Jesus the Overcomer
    E. Power of Forgiveness

II. Section #2: Living in Freedom
    A. The Triune Nature of Man: Body, Soul and Spirit
    B. The Destiny of Each Believer
    C. Biblical List of Sins
    D. Breaking the Bands that Bind

III. Section #3: Baptism in the Holy Spirit
    A. The Prophecy of the Holy Spirit
    B. The Promise of the Holy Spirit
    C. The Power of the Holy Spirit
    D. Jesus, the Baptizer of the Holy Spirit
    E. The Baptism in the Holy Spirit

IV. Section #4: Getting Grounded in Christ and Giving Your Testimony

    A. Getting Grounded
        1. Commitment to local church
        2. Cell ministry
        3. Water baptism
        4. Daily word
        5. Prayer
        6. Eliminate things related to sin
        7. Witness
        8. Servanthood

    B. Applying the Full Armor of God

    C. Writing and Sharing Your Testimony

Vision for a Family Building Church

INTRODUCTION

In Edward Gibbon's 1788 book *The Decline and Fall of the Roman Empire*, five basic reasons are set forth as to why that great civilization withered and died:

1. The undermining of the dignity and sanctity of the home, which is the basis of human society.
2. Higher and higher taxes, the spending of public money for free bread and circuses for the populace.
3. The mad craze for pleasure with sports and plays becoming more exciting, more brutal and more immoral.
4. The building of great armaments when the real enemy was within: the decay of individual responsibility.
5. The decay of religion and religious leaders who lost touch with life and their power to guide.

The decline and fall is not just like a story about some faraway nation; it is a reality about this nation NOW! There are many areas the enemy is attacking, but the family seems to be one of his primary targets. What will the enemy bring into your home in the next week, month or year to destroy from within? Who's knocking at your door? And more importantly, who is guarding the spiritual entrance to your home?

I. BUILDING A HOUSE THAT WILL STAND
(Matthew 7:24-27)

A. The Wise Builder
(Matthew 7:24-25)

1. Obedient to the Word (Matthew 7:24)
   Being shaped by:
   a. King Jesus, kingdom laws, word of God
   b. Godly, gifted ministries
   c. Godly friends, right values
   d. The Holy Spirit alive in the inner man

2. Proper Foundations (Matthew 7:24)
   a. Biblical convictions, belief in the Bible as a book of absolutes
   b. Belief in the family as the cornerstone of society
   c. Belief in God's rewards and judgements
   d. Belief in Christ as the only answer to life's dilemmas

3. Expects Storm and Fortifies House (Matthew 7:25)
   a. Rains
   b. Floods
   c. Winds
   d. Beat upon the house

B.   The Foolish Builder
(Matthew 7:26-27)

1.   Hearer but Not Doer (Matthew 7:26-27)

2.   Faulty, Weak Foundation (Matthew 7:26-27)
   a.   Public opinion
   b.   Christian approval
   c.   Accommodating theology
   d.   Acceptance by other wavering Christians
   e.   Delayed consequences

3.   Not Able to Stand Against Storms (Matthew 7:26-27)
"... and it fell and great was the fall of it..."
"... down it fell, it collapsed, and disastrous was the fall, mighty was the crash, and its downfall was complete..."

II.   GUARDING THE DOOR
(I Chronicles 9:19; Exodus 12:7,22-23; John 10:1-9)

A.   What Is The Door?
   1.   Spiritually speaking, the door represents those in spiritual authority in any household who are responsible for the spiritual health of the home.
   2.   Doorkeeper (Heb): To spread out, to cover, to preserve, guard, stand at the threshold

B.   Who Is At The Door?
   1.   Genesis 4:7 "Sin is crouching at the door and its desire is for you, but you must master it."
   2.   Exodus 12:23 "The destroyer is at the door."

III.   CLEANSING LEAVENING INFLUENCES FROM THE HOUSE
(Exodus 12:15-20; 13:7; I Corinthians 5:6-7; Zephaniah 1:12)

A.   The Definition of Leaven
   1.   Webster's Dictionary: "Anything that makes a general change in a mass, tempering the quality of a thing, to spread through causing a gradual change."
   2.   Dictionary of New Testament Theology: "Leaven is used symbolically as an evil influence which spreads like an infection."

B.   How Leaven Works
   1.   Leaven works secretly and silently.
   2.   Leaven works slowly and gradually.
   3.   Leaven works persistently until the whole is leavened.

C. Identifying Destructive Leavening Influences
   1. The leaven of Herod (Mark 6:14-18; 8:15)
   2. The leaven of Sadducees (Matthew 16:6-12)
   3. The leaven of Pharisees (Luke 12:1)
   4. The leaven of Corinth (I Corinthians 5:1-13)
   5. The leaven of Galatian Church (Galatians 5:9)

D. Modern Day Leaven/The World's Philosophical Conclusions

IV. DOORKEEPERS' RESPONSIBILITIES
(Matthew 24:43; Ephesians 6:10-12)

A. Parents as Doorkeepers to Their Children

   1. You must understand the principle of covering or umbrella principle over your children. If you as a parent allow moral failure, unrepented attitudes, deception, immoral viewing of television, etc., you open a leak in your protection for the family against Satan. Eli became an open door for Satan to destroy his family (I Samuel 3:4)

   2. You must present every child to God in consecration and lead them into dedication. Samuel was presented in the temple (I Samuel 2).

   3. You must cultivate a healthy fear of God in your children. God is watching and knows and judges accordingly (Proverbs 16:6)

   4. You must shepherd your children and lead them to God: salvation, baptism of the Holy Spirit, worship, prayer.

   5. You must train your children to recognize and resist the devil and youthful lusts (II Timothy 2:22)

   6. You must teach your children how to stand alone and not be dependent on friends or family, but on Jesus and His principles alone.

   7. You must pray daily for a hedge around your home and family. The enemy is crouching, ready to attack, waiting for any and every opportunity. You are the protection, the door. Job 1:10 says he made a hedge round about his house. Mark 3:27 commands us to bind the strong man.

   8. You must have daily family devotions to lead children in seeking God and His kingdom continually.

B. Husbands as Doorkeeper to Their Wives
   1. Purity of life
   2. Personal devotions

---

3. The servant-leader
4. Looking out for wife's interests
5. Financial security
6. Understanding her as a woman
7. Communication
8. Love her as Christ loves the church
9. Root our bitterness, anger, loose tongue

C. Christians as Doorkeepers to Their Own Lives
1. Personal and corporate prayer
2. Bible reading/study
3. Church involvement
4. Spirit-led life
5. 100% commitment to Christ
6. Forgive as Christ forgives

D. The Church as Doorkeeper to the Home
1. Sunday school
2. Camps and retreats
3. Home meetings
4. Counseling
5. Youth ministries
6. Solid Bible teaching

V. WHAT IS THE CHURCH'S RESPONSIBILITY TO FAMILY LIFE?

A. What attitude should the church have to the home?
1. Promote family unity
2. Family is the basic unit of the church. Strong family is essential to strong church.
3. Covering
4. The church is to serve the family. The family also needs to focus on how they can serve the church. Both need to focus on giving to the other.
5. Don't so emphasize family you overlook singles.

B. How can church practically serve family?
1. Preach and teach on family
2. Nursery and children's ministry
3. Special classes on marriage, parenting, blended families helping your teens make college/career choices
4. Equip people to care for aged parents
5. Help single moms in practical areas: big brothers, car repair, benevolence fund
6. Marriage life groups
7. Couple-to-couple mentoring
8. Blended families – accept, love and apply Bible to their special needs

Vision for a Business People Building Church

INTRODUCTION: The local church and the overseeing leadership must cultivate a biblical vision for those who are called to the marketplace. The businessperson is a vital key to spreading the gospel in the secular setting and to being a blessing to the local church. Business people usually have the gifts of faith, giving and leadership. These people need to be encouraged, challenged, accepted, respected, released and pastored.

> The Christian businessperson is a sign of the kingdom of God in this present world, called to cultivate a distinctiveness that points to the world's future and to live and work in the world's presence, called to be light, showing the life of the kingdom to the world, as salt permeating the world, a reflection of godly eternal values <u>in</u> the world and <u>to</u> the world.

I. THE BUSINESS PERSON AND THE "WORLD" TENSION

A. The Tension

WORLD	WORLD SYSTEM
Created by God for my stewardship, my use, my responsibility, my calling. I am fulfilled as I develop my work and service in this world *Ps 8:6; II Cor 5:19 Mk 16:15; Jn 17:11*	In its fallen for my state has powerful, subtle influences on our thinking and living. It can pervert our mind, motives and corrupt our simplicity toward Christ. *I Jn 5:19; I Cor 3:19; Jn 12:31; Col 2:8; Rom 12:2*

B. The Wise Business Person Identifies Worldliness
   (Jm 4:4; I Jn 2:15; II Tim 4:10; I John 3:1; 4:5; 5:4; 5:19)

   1. Worldiness is becoming like the fallen world system, or the spirit of this world. It is becoming one with the fallen worldly values, the philosophy of life, standards of morality, deceptive human philosophies, selfish ambition, covetousness, idolatrous worship of something other than God, the autonomous following of self-chosen goals.

   2. Worldliness is that attitude towards the world that makes the world a rival to the love and service of God because the world in this sense is deeply corrupted by sin and is described as under the control of the evil one.

3. Worldliness can be defined in giving service and loyalty to created things rather than to God and in loving them in the strong sense of giving them priority. It involves being diverted from the exclusive love and loyalty that are due to God alone by the attitudes, priorities and practices of our culture. Instead we are to overcome the world.

II. THE BUSINESS PERSON AND A VISION FOR SUCCESS
(Proverbs 10:22; 24:25)

A. The Biblical Words Every Business Person Should Know

1. *Blessing*: A benediction, prosperity; a gift; to speak well of, cause to prosper, make happy, bestow blessings on. A benediction in which happiness is foretold; that which promotes temporal prosperity or welfare (Gen 12:2; Deut 11:27; II Sam 7:29; Eph 1:3; Heb 6:7; II Cor 9:5-6)

2. *Honor*: weight, glory, honor, wealth, reputation; can emphasize the position of an individual within the sphere in which he lives; high esteem, respect, good name or reputation (Proverbs 11:16; Proverbs 26:1,8; 20:3; 25:2)

3. *Favor*: to be gracious and considerate toward, show favor; to show generosity toward; graciousness, benefit, favor; kind regard, benevolence shown by word or deed, partiality toward, to afford advantages for success, to facilitate (Genesis 33:5; Psalm 37:21; Luke 1:30: 2:52)

4. *Delight*: to be pleased with, desire; take pleasure in, take care of; to rejoice in and with, to delight with someone in something; A high degree of pleasure or joy, to receive great pleasure in. Delight is more permanent than joy and not dependent on sudden excitement. (Proverbs 8:35; 11:27; 11:1; 22:9; 12:22; 12:2; 15:8; Romans 7:22)

5. *Prosperous*: Succeed, prosper, have a successful venture; break out, be profitable; to help on one's way, to have a prosperous journey; advancing in the pursuit of any thing desirable; making gain or increase; thriving; successful (Genesis 24:21; II Chronicles 26:5; I Corinthians 16:2; 3 John 2)

6. *Success*: to be prudent, act wisely, give attention to, prosper; the favorable or prosperous termination of any thing attempted (Deuteronomy 29:9; Joshua 1:7-8; I Kings 2:3)

B.   True Success

    1.   Fulfilling the purposes for which God has created you. It is accomplishing the dreams God has had for you from before the foundations of the world.

    2.   Is a journey, a gradual process, avoiding extremes that damage biblical values and balanced living.

    3.   Earl Nightingale, a philosopher, wrote in <u>The Strangest Secret</u> "Success is the progressive realization of a worthy ideal." It is not IQ, education, age, race, birth, money or power. It doesn't mean getting there, being there, having it all, fame or fortune, looking down from the summit, being with the "in crowd."

III.   THE BUSINESS PERSON AND A BIBLICAL PHILOSOPHY OF SUCCESS

A.   We are to extend the kingdom of God. We are to live with a goal toward excellence and an attitude of achievement toward biblical success, biblical values and biblical priorities.
(Genesis 1:26-28)

B.   We are to adopt the early Protestant or Puritan work ethic. This is a simple view in which the average person believes his or her work not only matters but contributes to a sense of community and integrity in all of life.
(I Thessalonians 3:6-10; 5:12; I Corinthians 4:12; 15:16; Colossians 1:29; Philippians 2:16; Isaiah 65:21-22)

C.   We must adopt the view that it is our Christian duty to transcend mediocrity in our daily routines and link our work in the world with our service to an all-knowing God of excellence who desires believers to work with excellence and achieve success in our area of responsibility. This is our divine calling.
(Ephesians 6:5-8; II Timothy 1:9; II Peter 1:10; Ephesians 4:1)

D.   We must adopt the biblical view that God has a destiny for me which He has known in advance and is wisely directing my life toward. This destiny involves my calling to be a success in my work. My everyday ordinary life has within it seeds of greatness.
(Romans 8:28-30; Jeremiah 1:5; Psalm 139:15; Ephesians 4:14)

IV. THE BUSINESS PERSON'S CHALLENGE: GOD'S WAY OR MAN'S WAY

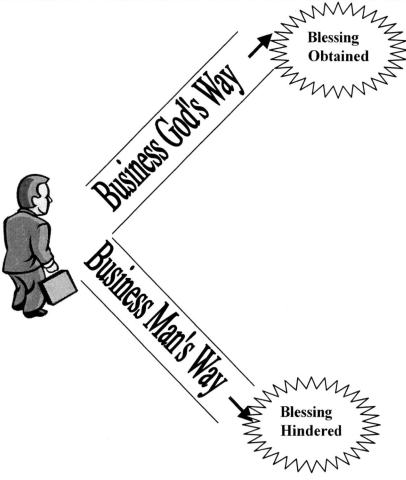

V. THE BUSINESS PERSON'S NEVER GIVE UP PROCLAMATION
(Matt 24:13; Prov 24:10; Josh 6:1-5; Isa 42:5; Isa 43:5; James 5:10)

> "Today's mighty oak is yesterday's little nut that held its ground."
>
> "The highest reward for man's toil is not what he gets for it but what he becomes by it."

A. Never give up on the dream God put in your heart.
(Gen 37:1-10; Prov 13:12; Prov 4:23; Deut 1:21; Judg 6:11-14)

B. Never give up on the specific prayers you have been praying.
(Lk 18:1-7; James 5:15-17; 2 Chr 26:5)

C. Never give up on attaining the blessing, favor and honor of God on your business.
(Prov 8:35; Prov 10:22; Prov 11:27; 3 Jn 1:2)

D.   Never give up on conquering the spiritual strongholds that resist your success.
     (Jer 6:1-5; Song 2:15)

E.   Never give up on giving liberally, especially in hard times.
     (Mal 3:9-12; 2 Cor 9:5-6; Prov 22:9; 1 Cor 16:2)

F.   Never give up when discouraged because of fiery trials.
     (I Pet 1:6; II Sam 23:20-21)

G.   Never give up when mistreated by people who surprise you.
     (II Tim 4:11; Heb 12:3)

H.   Never give up on staying planted and involved in your local church.
     (Prov 24:30; Ps 1:1-3; Ps 92:13)

I.   Never give up on living and leading by integrity, even when it doesn't seem to pay off.
     (Prov 11:1,18; 12:22; 13:22; Dan 5:12,14,16; I Kings 9:4; Ps 41:12)

J.   Never give up because of apparent lack of fruit or results.
     (Hab 3:17-19; Rom 8:28; Gal 6:9)

K.   Never give up because of the impossible odds.
     (II Sam 23:9-12; II Tim 4:5-8)

L.   Never give up when the enemy wins a fight; he won't win the war.
     (I Sam 30:1-10)

M.   Never give up when you make mistakes or fail; get up again.
     (Micah 7:7-8; Prov 24:16)

"Keep your eye on the end result, the outcome, the finished product."

Vision for a Word Church

INTRODUCTION: The Bible teaches us that we are to come under the word of God as we are also responsible to get into the word of God. God has ordained teachers to teach. God calls, equips and anoints those gifted ministries in the local church. The very first thing Jesus did after His ascension was to give gifts to the church. (Eph 4:11-12) The prophet Isaiah prophesies about the last days and the house of the Lord being built. In that house there would be teaching. (Isa 2:3; Micah 4:2)

I.   **HEBREWS 4:12**

New King James: For the <u>word of God</u> is living and powerful, and sharper than any two-edged sword, piercing even to the division of soul and spirit, and of joints and marrow, and is a discerner of the thoughts and intents of the heart.

Amplified: For the <u>Word that God speaks</u> is alive and full of power [making it active, operative, energizing, and effective]; it is sharper than any two-edged sword, penetrating to the dividing line of the breath of life (soul) and [the immortal] spirit, and of joints and marrow [of the deepest parts of our nature], exposing and sifting and analyzing and judging the very thoughts and purposes of the heart.

The Message: <u>His powerful word</u> is sharp as a surgeon's scalpel, cutting through everything, whether doubt or defense, laying us open to listen and obey. Nothing and no one is impervious to God's word. We can't get away from it—no matter what.

A.   The Word of God

1.   This is the spoken and written word of God and cannot be taken lightly. If the read doer not listen, he or she faces God himself. The word demands a response. God does not tolerate indifference. (Jn 10:35; Lk 16:17; II Tim 3:16; Rom 3:2; Acts 7:38)

2.   The authority of scripture is the authority of Jesus Christ; they are indivisible. To attempt to distinguish the two is like asking which blade of a pair of scissors is more important, or which leg of a pair of pants is more necessary. We know Christ through the Bible and we understand the Bible through the knowledge of Christ; the two cannot be separated. That is why Paul calls it "the word of Christ." (Ray Stedman)

B.   The Word is Living
"God's Message is a living and active power (TCNT), the Divine Reason (Wade) is alive and full of power in action (Williams), lives and is active (Becky) and workable (Klingensmith) and energetic (Wilson)."[1]

---

[1] Ralph W. Harris, ed. *The New Testament Study Bible Hebrews-Jude.* Springfield, MO: The Complete Biblical Library, 1986. Page 53.

C. The Word is Active, Energetic, Powerful
(John 1:12; Philippians 3:21; Colossians 1:29)
"God's Message is a living and active power (TCNT), the Divine Reason (Wade) is alive and full of power in action (Williams), lives and is active (Becky) and workable (Klingensmith) and energetic (Wilson)."[2]

D. The Word is Sharper, Cutting From and Into
(Eph 6:17; Rev 1:16; Isa 49:2)
Keener than any two-edged blade (Wade) and more cutting than any two-edged sword (Wilson), any double-edged sword (Williams), a sword that cuts both ways (NLT).[3]

E. The Word is Piercing, Penetrating and Dividing
(1 Thes 5:23; 1 Cor 15:45)
It can slice between (SEB). It is a judge of (Klingensmith), penetrating deeply enough to split soul and spirit (Adams) cutting through even to a separation of life and breath (Wilson), even to the severance of soul from spirit (Montgomery).[4]

F. The Word Judges Thoughts and Intentions of the Heart
(Ps 139:1-3,12; Jn 12:47-48)
"It is keen in judging the thoughts (Norlie). It can tell the difference between the desires and the intentions of the human mind (SEB) and detecting the inmost thoughts (TCNT) and is a sifter and analyzer of the reflections and conceptions of the heart (Wuest). It is a judge of the sentiments and thoughts of the heart (Concordant), the very thoughts (Montgomery).

II. **BALANCED MINISTRY OF JESUS AND THE EARLY CHURCH**
(Matthew 4:23; 9:35)

A. The Three-Fold Cord of Jesus' Ministry
Stretching from the inception of the Christian faith down to this very hour, there is an unbroken succession of teachers. Wherever preaching was at its best, the sermons (as exemplified in the sermons of Peter, Stephen, and Paul) contain a large element of teaching content.
1. Teaching: systematic instruction (used 217 times)
2. Preaching: anointed proclamation (used 140 times)
3. Healing: supernatural works of the Holy Spirit.

---

[2] Ralph W. Harris, ed. *The New Testament Study Bible Hebrews-Jude.* Springfield, MO: The Complete Biblical Library, 1986. Page 53.
[3] Harris, page 53.
[4] Harris, page 54.

B. Jesus: The Teacher
Jesus was frequently called "Rabbi" or "Teacher." Of the ninety times the Lord was addressed, as recorded in the gospels, sixty times he was called "Rabbi". Furthermore, the thought of the speaker in at least part of the thirty remaining cases was directed toward Jesus as a teacher, for the Greek word *didaskalos*, which refers to "one who teaches concerning the things of God and the duties of man," is translated sometimes "teacher" and sometimes "master."

C. The First Church Emphasized Continual Teaching
(Acts 5:42; Acts 6:7; Acts 11:26; Acts 15:35; Acts 20:20; Acts 28:31; Acts 13:1)

D. Effects of Teaching in the Early Church
There is no question but that the teacher was the central figure of the first century church. In this age of many books and much use of the radio and television, it is rather difficult to appreciate fully how successfully the apostles and their successors carried on by means of an oral ministry. Textbooks were unknown; even the record of the words and works of the Lord Jesus were not committed to writing until thirty years after His resurrection. But the apostolic church was the burning expression of personalities who had been made new creatures in Christ Jesus and who went everywhere teaching the good news. The eminent church historian, Philip, Schaff, gives tribute to the place and importance of the teaching ministry in the early church in the following words: "It is a remarkable fact that after the days of the Apostles no great missionaries are mentioned until the Middle Ages. There were no missionary societies, no missionary institutions, no organized efforts in the ante-Nicean age. Yet in less than 300 years after the death of the disciple John, the whole population of the Roman empire, which then represented the civilized world, was nominally Christianized.

E. Teaching in the Church of Later Days
It is very evident that the work of the teacher in the past was, and continues to be in the present, the bulwark of the Roman Catholic Church. Both Protestant and Catholic historians agree that the religious school machinery the Jesuits set in motion as a counter movement to the Protestant Reformation arrested its triumphant advance. When Protestantism threatened to sweep Catholicism from the face of Europe, Ignatius Loyola and Francis Xavier conceived the plan of reaching the children and rearing up a new generation of lovers and defenders of Roman doctrine. The effective tools of the Jesuits were not the inquisition chambers, but their schools. The Jesuit priests stated, "Give me a child until he is six years old and then you may have him." Those Protestant denominations which have recognized the place and importance of teaching have also been signally successful. Government statistics show that in the decade ending in 1926 the Lutherans added a larger proportion of pupils to their Sunday schools than any other denomination except the Southern Baptist Church. Prior to 1900, the Southern Baptist Convention had never emphasized the teaching ministry. One of its members said at that time, "We have

organized; we have evangelized; we have preached, but we have never taught." It was in 1900 that Dr. J.B. Gambrel, the president of the Convention, declared, "The time has come for us to further the teaching ministry. I believe the most significant of all modern movements it he work of teacher training. Upon his recommendation, the denomination adopted the slogan, "A certificate for every teacher" and began to concentrate all its resources upon the preparation of Sunday school teachers for their task. Since that time, teacher training has been stressed on every platform and in every paper with the result that the Sunday School Board is now issuing more than a hundred thousand awards annually.
(C.B. Eavey, Principles of Teaching for Christian Teachers)

III. BIBLICAL WORDS USED TO DESCRIBE THE TEACHING PROCESS

A. Old Testament Terms

1. **Discipline**: lamadh. To beat. A very common word for "to teach", it may have meant "to beat with a rod, to chastise and may have originally referred to the striking and goading of beasts by which they were curbed and trained. By a noble evolution the term came to describe the process of disciplining and training men in war, religion and life (Is 2:3; Hos 10:11; Micah 4:2).

2. **Law**: yarah. To cast. The teaching idea from which the law was derived is expressed by a very which means to throw, to cast as an arrow or lot. It is also used of thrusting the hand forth to point out or show clearly (Gen 46:28; Exodus 15:25). The original ideas is easily changed into an educational conception since the teacher puts forth new ideas and facts as a sower casts seed into the ground.

3. **Discernment**: bin. To separate. To cause to distinguish or separate. The word meaning "to separate or to distinguish" is often used in a causative sense to signify "to teach".

4. **Wisdom**: sakhal. To be wise. The verb from which the various nominal forms for "wisdom" are derived means "to look at, to behold, to view" and in the causative stem describes the process by which one is enabled to see for himself what had never before entered his physical or intellectual field of consciousness. The noun indicates a wise person or sage whose mission is to instruct others in the ways of the Lord (Proverbs 16:23).

5. **Knowledge**: yadha. To see. This verb literally means to see and consequently to perceive, to know, to come to know and cause to know or teach. It describes the act of knowing as both progressive and completed.

6. ***Illumination***: *zahar*. To shine. This verbal root signifies "to shine, to bring to light" and when applied to the intellectual sphere indicates the function of teaching to be one of illumination. Ignorance is darkness, knowledge is light. Moses was to teach the people statutes and laws or to enlighten them on the principles and precepts of God's revelation (Ex 18:20).

7. ***Vision***: *ra'-ah*. To see. The literal meaning of this very is "to see" and the nominal form is the ancient name for prophet or authoritative teacher who was expected to have a clear vision of spiritual realities, the will of God, the need of man and the way of life (I Sam 9:9; I Chr 9:22; 2 Chr 16:7).

8. ***Inspiration***: *nabha*. To boil up. The most significant word for "prophet" is derived from the verb which means "to boil up or forth like a fountain" and consequently to pour forth words under the impelling power of the spirit of God.

9. ***Nourishment***: *ra`ah*. To feed a flock. The name "shepherd", so precious in both the Old and New Testaments, comes from a verb meaning "to feed" hence to protect and care for out of a sense of devotion, ownership and responsibility. It is employed with reference to civil rulers in their positions of trust (II Sam 5:2; Jer 23:2), with reference to teachers of virtue and wisdom (Pr 10:21; Eccl 12;11), and preeminently with reference to God as the great Shepherd of His chosen people (Ps 23:1).

B. New Testament Terms

1. ***Instruction***: *didasko*. To teach. The usual word for "teach" in the New Testament signifies either to hold a discourse with others in order to instruct them or to deliver a didactic discourse where there may not be direct personal and verbal participation. In the former sense it describes the interlocutory method, the interplay of the ideas and words between pupils and teachers, and in the latter use it refers to the more formal monologues designed especially to give information (Matthew 4:23; 13:36; John 6:59; I Cor 4:17; I Tim 2:12).

2. ***Acquisition***: *Manthano*. To learn. The central thought of teaching is causing one to learn. Teaching and learning are not scholastic but dynamic and imply personal relationship and activity in the acquisition of knowledge (Mt 11:29; 28:19; Acts 14:21).

3. ***Presentation***: *paratithemi*. To place beside.

4. ***Elucidation***: *diermeneuo*. To interpret. The work of interpreter is to make truth clear an to effect the edification of the hearer (Lk 24:27; I Cor 12;30; 14:5,13,27).

5. ***Exposition***: *ektithemi*. To place out. The verb literally means "to set or place out" and signifies to bring out the latent and secret ideas of a literary passage or a system of thought and life.

IV. BIBLICAL RESULTS OF BIBLICAL TEACHING

A. Biblical Teaching Not Human Reasoning

B. Biblical Results Expected
1. Divine guidance in life (Ps 119:105; Ps 119:133)
2. Spiritual cleansing from all things that hinder (Ps 119:9; Ps 119:11)
3. Spiritual health and vitality (Prov 4:4; Prov 4:20-22)
4. Security and safety (Ps 18:30; Ps 19:8)
5. Established in foundational truths (Heb 5:12-14; Heb 6:1-3; 1 Pet 1:12)
6. Equipped for the work of the Lord (Eph 4:11-13)
7. Darkness driven out (1 Pet 2:9; I Jn 1:6-7)
8. Instruction in the principles of warfare (Ps 18:34; Ps 144:1)

Vision for a Principle-Driven Church

INTRODUCTION: Without a doubt, we are living in some of the most exciting days of our lives. Yet along with the excitement there is always the potential that could be devastating. Living on the edge of what God is doing is challenging. We as leaders have heard a particular call of the Spirit, an urge to get involved and with the Holy Spirit build the local church. What a terrific call! What a way to live, that is if we live within God's guidelines, His eternal principles.

I. **MULTIPLE VOICES: A TIME TO BE CAREFUL**
    (I Corinthians 14:7-8; Psalm 29:3-9; Ecclesiastes 5:3; II Peter 2:16; Jeremiah 5:31)

    A.   Discerning What's Behind a Voice

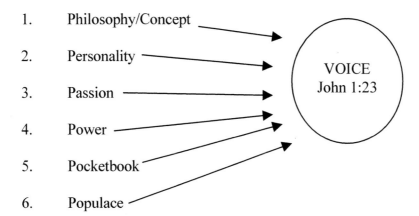

        1.   Philosophy/Concept

        2.   Personality

        3.   Passion

        4.   Power

        5.   Pocketbook

        6.   Populace

    B.   Multiple Voices
        1.   Dallas Theological Seminary
        2.   Kingdom Now
        3.   Reconstructionists, Replacement Theology
        4.   Foursquare
        5.   Bill Hybels
        6.   Vineyard
        7.   Covenant Church
        8.   Prophetic Movement
        9.   Church Growth
        10. Feed the Hungry
        11. Warfare
        12. Missions Agencies
        13. Restoration, Latter Rain
        14. Television that appears to be Christian

        MOTIF: "Overall main emphasis that is spoken or unspoken but it is the shaping invisible force behind everything."

C.   Reaction Attitudes to Avoid

    1.   Attitude of defensiveness

    2.   Attitude of spiritual pride

    3.   Attitude of rejection without inspection

    4.   Attitude of persecutor: persecute the other movement

II.   SPIRITUAL DISCERNMENT: KEY TO LEADERSHIP LONGEVITY
(I Corinthians 12:10; I Kings 3:9-11; Matthew 16:3-5)

A.   Sound Judgement - Need for Balance

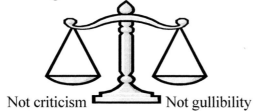

Not criticism   Not gullibility

B.   Sources of True Discernment

    1.   Doctrine - The foundation for discernment

    2.   Direction - The focus for discernment

    3.   Discipline - The emotion of discernment

    4.   Diagnosis - The work of discernment

III.   PRINCIPLES: KEY TO LOCAL CHURCH LONGEVITY

A.   Knowing the Difference Between Principles, Trends and Methods

    1.   Principle
        a.   A guiding sense of the obligation of right conduct
        b.   A comprehensive and fundamental law, doctrine or assumption
        c.   An unchangeable law that is timeless and will work in any generation
        d.   A conviction; a life producing truth that conquers you

    2.   Trend: A current style or preference, taste

    3.   Methods: A way, technique or process of or for doing something; could be temporary or conditional

B. Identifying Biblical Principles
    1. Principles are based on eternal values as seen in the Word of God.
    2. Principles are an extension of God's character as applied in any circumstance at any time.
    3. Principles are derived from biblical history and basic theology as presented in both Old and New Testament.
    4. Principles are usually evident within certain biblical models such as the Tabernacle of Moses, the Levitical priesthood and the conquering of Canaan.
    5. Principles must become convictions.

C. Difference Between Principles and Methods
    1. A principle is an extension of biblical truth; truth does not change. A method is an extension of personality, culture, spiritual roots, strategy. Method is an application of principle.
    2. As principle passes through method, it may or may not be weakened, strengthened, obscured, changed or even forgotten. We must be careful to maintain the integrity of truth and yet use methods that are effective and culturally easy to embrace.

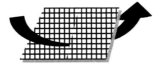

D. Essential Principles Needed to Build Churches That Last

    1. The Hub Principle: "Working from the whole to the part and the part back to the whole"

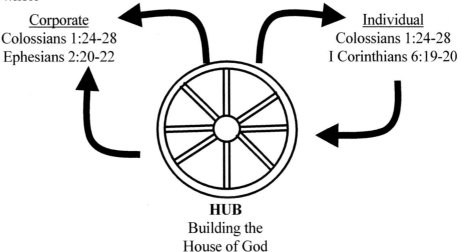

Corporate
Colossians 1:24-28
Ephesians 2:20-22

Individual
Colossians 1:24-28
I Corinthians 6:19-20

HUB
Building the
House of God
Ephesians 3:10-11; Ephesians 5:25-31; I Corinthians 12:12-30
Ephesians 4:12-16; Matthew 16:18

The corporate expression exists to express the life of God in community as well as for the betterment and release of individual believers. The individual expression exists to express the life of God in a single person as well as for the sake of the corporate good.

2.   "The Objective Rules the Subjective" Principle

3.   "The Clear Interprets the Obscure" Principle

4.   "The Minor Emphasis is Submitted to the Major Emphasis" Principle

5.   "The Proven Basics Take Preeminence Over the Unknown Success Ideas" Principle

6.   The Cross Principle

7.   The Team Principle

8.   The Biblical Blueprint Principle

9.   "The Unity With Diversity Without Confusion" Principle

10.   The Single Vision Principle

11.   "The Harmony and Unity of Leadership" Principle

12.   The Prayer Principle

13.   The Presence of God Principle

14.   The Authority Principle

15.   The Commitment and Serving Principle

IV.   THE DANGER OF ROUTINE INEFFECTIVENESS

A.   Routine can settle in almost imperceptibly in such a way that God's purpose for His church is assumed and therefore neglected. Ineffectiveness occurs more often by default than by intention.

B.   Dangers Discerned
1.   Organism into organization
2.   Community into association
3.   Mission orientation into maintenance orientation
4.   Fellowship into formality
5.   Function into form
6.   Success seeking into survival seeking
7.   Pursuit of accomplishment into pursuit of convenience
8.   Discipleship into churchmanship
9.   The work of the church into church work
10.   Leadership into bureaucracy
11.   Team members into spectators or clients
12.   Purpose into routine repetition

Vision for a Gifts Functioning Church

I Corinthians 12:1-14:40

INTRODUCTION: It is important to emphasize that the context for the gifts of the Spirit was the experience of the Spirit's outpouring. Without this there would not have been vitality and power sufficient for the gifts to be manifested and multiplied. Let it be firmly said that the church cannot be fully and freely the church without the presence and operation of the gifts of the Holy Spirit. What is depicted here in I Corinthians 12-14 and recurring in our day is in no sense a peripheral matter, but is crucial to the life of the church. For the recurrence of the gifts of the Holy Spirit signals the church's recovery of its spiritual roots and its emergence in the 20th century with fresh power and vitality. The devil's strategy is to cause us to be passive, to live in boredom with no need to function. God's strategy is supernatural, a living, whole church.

I Cor 12:1-14:40   Pauline Theology on Spiritual Activity in the Local Church

     12:      The Pneumatic Charismata Gifts Listed in General
     13:      The Exercise of Gifts through the Power of Love
     14:      The Order of Charismatic Services, Prophecy and Tongues

I. THE LEADER'S RESPONSIBILITY IN ESTABLISHING GIFTS IN THE LOCAL CHURCH

A.   Teach on spiritual gifts.

B.   Help people identify their spiritual gifts.

C.   Equip the people for placement.

D.   Place them in ministry, opening doors of opportunity for them.

E.   Give them ongoing oversight.

II. PROCESS OF DEVELOPING THE GIFTS

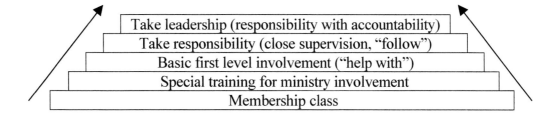

Take leadership (responsibility with accountability)
Take responsibility (close supervision, "follow")
Basic first level involvement ("help with")
Special training for ministry involvement
Membership class

III. FIVE BASIC PRESUPPOSITIONS ON SPIRITUAL GIFTS

A. Every believer has a destiny to fulfill.
(Romans 8:28-30)

B. Every believer must dedicate himself to this destiny.
(Romans 12:1-2)

C. Every believer should be enlightened concerning the origin, history and biblical basis of spiritual gifts.
(I Corinthians 12:1)

D. The believer will not be able to operate in spiritual gifts successfully or powerfully unless a strong spiritual flow is constantly maintained.
(John 7:37-39; II Kings 3:19,25; Genesis 26:18-19)

E. Spiritual gifts are rooted in the grace of God and operate best by the love of God flowing freely through imperfect people.
(I Corinthians 12:9; 14:1; 12:4; Romans 12:6; I Peter 4:10; Ephesians 4:7)

IV. FIVE BASIC SCRIPTURAL TRUTHS ON SPIRITUAL GIFTS

A. Scripture teaches that the believer has received the gift of the Holy Spirit,
(Acts 2:38; John 3:6; Ephesians 1:13)

B. Scripture teaches that the believer has received certain gifts of the Holy Spirit.
(I Corinthians 12:4; Romans 12:6; Colossians 2:10; I Peter 4:10-11; I Timothy 4:14; II Timothy 1:6-7)

C. Scripture establishes a difference between natural talents and spiritual gifts.
(I Corinthians 1:19-26; Matthew 25; Isaiah 43:7; Ephesians 4:7-8)

D. Scripture teaches that gifts of the Spirit are not on the same level of authority or infallibility as the written word of God.
(II Timothy 3:15-16; I Corinthians 14:29; 13:9-10,12)

E. Scripture teaches the purpose of gifts is for ministry and service.
(I Corinthians 14:12)

NOT:
1. To draw attention to man or satisfy ego
2. For self-gratification or glorification
3. To prove a person's spirituality or maturity
4. Marked by flamboyant or spectacular manifestations but by dedicated service

V.   THE IGNORANCE PROBLEM

I Corinthians 12:1 "Now concerning spiritual things, concerning those who exercise spiritual gifts, I do not want you ignorant."

A.   The New Testament Meaning of Ignorance

    1.   Now concerning: This expression appears six times in I Corinthians and each time addresses a concern raised by the Corinthians themselves (7:1; 7:25; 8:1; 16:1; 12:1; 10:1).

    2.   Ignorant: (Gr) agnoeo = not to know, be ignorant, not to understand, ignore something of importance or disregard. (Romans 1:13; 10:3; 11:25; I Corinthians 10:1; 12:1; 14:38; I Thessalonians 4:13)

        a.   It is diverse in meaning and can indicate a deficiency or lapse of intellectual ability or resources, to forget or misunderstand.

        b.   It may also suggest a misguided perception or a wrong response or wrong action, to act wrongly toward something out of ignorance.

        c.   It may mean (as in the Old Testament) sins of ignorance, unintentional or the simple lack of information and knowledge.

        d.   In the Pauline writings, to "not know" does not simply involve a lack of intellectual ability; it is not merely a cognitive function. Enlightenment is needed, spiritual illumination, spiritual teaching concerning spiritual things.

B.   The Ignorance of Church History and Spiritual Gifts
After the Apostolic Era problems of heresy and schism challenged the post-New Testament church. The church responded to these threats by developing its creeds, its canon of scripture and its clergy. As it struggled for institutional stability, the church neglected to teach about the power of the Holy Spirit and the gifts of the Spirit received little attention.

    1.   ***MONTANISTS MOVEMENT: 200 AD/2nd Century:*** The Montanists attempted to bring spiritual renewal and emphasized the gifts, leading to excessive supernaturalism, emotionalism, and fanaticism. The church over-reacted as church leaders were inclined to suspect those who claimed to experience any direct working of the Holy Spirit. Church officials became fearful of spiritual excesses and unbridled enthusiasm. They preferred order to what they regarded as chaos of spirituality of the Montanists Movement. This set a precedent we never really recovered from.

    2.   ***AUGUSTINE:*** Augustine represented the typical attitude toward spiritual gifts. He never really discussed them, was very vague in mentioning them and didn't see any real place for the gifts. He made them as anything common, natural talents of all.

3.	***THOMAS AQUINAS:*** Aquinas was a monk who was the representative theological of the Roman Catholic Church. He equated spiritual gifts with inner spiritual virtues we all have like love and hope. His views became standard for the Catholic church.

4.	***MARTIN LUTHER:*** Luther was a monk in the Protestant Reformation. When Luther discussed spiritual gifts, he identified them with talents or material blessings. Luther said to read other languages was a spiritual gift.

5.	***JOHN CALVIN:*** Calvin was a French theologian who said, "It does not appear that Paul intended here to mention those miraculous graces by which Christ at first rendered illustrations of His gospel, but on the contrary we find that he refers only to ordinary gifts such as were to continue perpetually in the church — natural God-given talents. Supernatural gifts of the Holy Spirit ceased with the death of the last apostle." John Wesley agreed.

6.	***REFORMED THEOLOGY:*** "The extraordinary gifts belonged to the extraordinary office of the apostles and showed themselves only in connection with that office." They were the foundation to fundamentalism, standing for the concreteness of scripture, not experiences. Reformed theology questioned those who seem to go to subjective experiences for their authority. They are dispensationalists who believe gifts went out with the last apostle and are not for today.

7.	***PENTECOSTAL MOVEMENT:*** The Pentecostal movement emphasized only a few of the spiritual gifts, especially tongues and healing. In fact, it became known as the "tongues movement." They never developed a theology of the spiritual gifts. Personal experience, emotionalism and shallow theology gave way to some extreme uses of the gifts, resulting in further rejection by the religious academic community. The Azusa Street Revival took place in 1906 followed by the 1948 Revival and Latter Rain with an emphasis on worship and prophetic gifts. Extremes developed here as well, but eventually truths were rediscovered.

8.	***CHARISMATIC MOVEMENT:*** In the last three decades there has been a new openness in the mainline denominations to the Holy Spirit and the gifts of the Holy Spirit which resulted in a charismatic church movement. Charismata is the Greek word for gifts. There was a new openness to some gifts, not all, and to the baptism of the Holy Spirit, but without the necessity of speaking in tongues. There was a real mixture of basic theology concerning the Holy Spirit and gifts and tongues called the "Third Wave" in some places: Roman Catholics, Presbyterians, Episcopalians, Baptists, Lutheran. Tony Campolo authored a book "How To Be Pentecostal Without Speaking in Tongues." A new terminology must be coped with: speaking in tongues, having the gift of prophecy, having a word from the Lord.

9. ***CITY BIBLE CHURCH:*** We are a unique blending of several spiritual movements, theologies and experiences. We have historic Pentecostal roots with a Latter Rain influence in our style of worship (spontaneous praise, belief in the five-fold ministries, presbytery and pre-service prayer) with a strong Baptist-type conviction for the authority of scripture, divine order in our public services and an evangelical "missionary zeal" to reach the world. We are not your typical Pentecostal church.

IV. THE GIFTS IN THE NEW TESTAMENT

A. **Prophecy**: Receive and communicate an immediate message of God to His people through a divinely-anointed utterance.

B. **Service**: Identify the unmet needs involved in a task related to God's work, and to make use of available resources to meet those needs and to help accomplish the desired goals.

C. **Teaching**: Communicate information relevant to the health and ministry of the Body and its members in such a way that others will learn.

D. **Exhortation**: Minister words of comfort, consolation, encouragement and counsel to other members of the Body in such a way that they feel helped and healed.

E. **Giving**: Contribute their material resources to the work of the Lord with liberality and cheerfulness.

F. **Leadership**: Set goals in accordance with God's purpose for the future and to communicate these goals to others in such a way that they voluntarily and harmoniously work together to accomplish those goals for the glory of God.

G. **Mercy**: Feel genuine empathy and compassion for individuals, both Christian and non-Christian, who suffer distressing physical, mental or emotional problems, and to translate that compassion into cheerfully-done deeds that reflect Christ's love and alleviate the suffering.

H. **Wisdom**: Know the mind of the Holy Spirit in such a way as to receive insight into how given knowledge may best be applied to specific needs arising in the Body of Christ.

I. **Knowledge**: Discover, accumulate, analyze and clarify information and ideas that are pertinent to the growth and well-being of the Body.

J. **Faith**: Discern with extraordinary confidence the will and purposes of God for the future of His work.

K. **Healing**: Serve as human intermediaries through whom it pleases God to cure illness and restore health apart from the use of natural means.

L. **Miracles**: Serve as human intermediaries through whom it pleases God to perform powerful acts that are perceived by observers to have altered the ordinary course of nature.

M. **Discerning of spirits**: Know with assurance whether certain behavior purported to be of God is in reality divine, human or satanic.

N. **Tongues**: to speak to God in a language they have never learned and/or to receive and communicate an immediate message of God to His people through a divinely-appointed utterance in a language they have never learned.

O. **Interpretation**: Make known in the vernacular the message of one who speaks in tongues.

P. **Apostle**: Assume and exercise general leadership over a number of churches with an extraordinary authority in spiritual matters that is spontaneously recognized and appreciated by those churches.

Q. **Helps**: Invest the talents they have in the life and ministry of other members of the Body, thus enabling the person helped to increase the effectiveness of his or her spiritual gifts.

R. **Administration**: Understand clearly the immediate and long-range goals of a particular unit of the Body of Christ and to devise and execute effective plans for the accomplishment of those goals.

S. **Evangelist**: Share the gospel with unbelievers in such a way that men and women become Jesus' disciples and responsible members of the Body of Christ.

T. **Pastor**: Assume a long-term personal responsibility for the spiritual welfare of a group of believers.

U. **Celibacy**: Remain single and enjoy it; to be unmarried and not suffer undue sexual temptations.

V. **Voluntary poverty**: Renounce material comfort and luxury and adopt a personal life-style equivalent to those living at the poverty level in a given society in order to serve God more effectively.

W. **Martyrdom**: Undergo suffering for the faith even to death while consistently displaying a joyous and victorious attitude that brings glory to God.

X. **Hospitality**: Provide open house and warm welcome for those in need of food and lodging.

Y. **Missionary**: Minister whatever other spiritual gifts they have in a second culture.

Z. **Intercession**: Pray for extended periods of time on a regular basis and see frequent and specific answers to their prayers to a degree much greater than that which is expected of the average Christian.

AA. **Exorcism**: Cast out demons and evil spirits.

Vision for a People Reaching Church

INTRODUCTION: A Harvesting Church theology will be developed by studying the harvest theme in the nine covenants of the Scripture, the Old Testament prophets, the Gospels, Pauline theology, and the Book of Revelation. A proper theological foundation is necessary for a proper ecclesiology and eschatology, all of which affects the vision of the church for the reaping of the harvest.

I.   THE IMPORTANCE OF HARVEST THEOLOGY

A.   Harvest Theology Determines Our Preaching

B.   Harvest Theology Determines Our Lifestyle

C.   Harvest Theology Determines Our Giving

D.   Harvest Theology Determines Prayer Life

E.   Harvest Theology Determines Values

II.   THE HARVEST FORETOLD IN THE COVENANTS

A.   Covenantal Theology Established
In the light of the all embracing revelation of God's covenants, the Bible is not to be viewed merely as a compilation of 66 books, but is rather to be seen as one book having one author with a progression of thought throughout. God being the author of all scripture, the progressive revelation of his covenantal dealings with man moves throughout the books of the Bible. The cross becomes the covenantal filter by which all covenants pass through. Covenantal theology is based on the covenantal principle of working from the part to the whole and the whole back to the part. The student must have an understanding of the covenants as a whole to interpret the part, but he must interpret the parts in order to realize the whole.

B.   The Covenants Promise Harvest
1.   Edenic Covenant (Genesis 1:26-28)
2.   Noahic Covenant (Genesis 9:1,7; 8:15-17; Jonah 15:16; Acts 9:31)
3.   Abrahamic Covenant (Genesis 12:2; 13:16; 15:5; 17:4-8; 22:17-18; 17:16)
4.   Davidic Covenant (II Samuel 7; I Chronicles 17; Psalm 89; Psalm 132; Jeremiah 33; II Chronicles 2:1; Ephesians 2:19-22; I Timothy 3:15)
5.   New Covenant (Matthew 26:26-30; Mark 14:22-26; Luke 22:17-20)

III. THE HARVEST FORESHADOWED IN THE FEASTS

A. The Feasts - Historical and Prophetical
(Deuteronomy 16:16-17; I Corinthians 15:46-47; Psalm 89:15)

First Month	Third Month	Seventh Month
Passover • Unleavened Bread • First Fruits Barley Harvest	Pentecost Wheat Harvest	Tabernacles • Trumpets • Day of Atonement • Tabernacles Fruit Harvest

B. The Feasts of Tabernacles - Last Day Harvest
(Leviticus 23:23-44)

   1. Feasts at the end of the year

   2. Feasts with the blowing of trumpets (Revelation 1:10; 10:7; 22:15-19; Matthew 24:3; I Thessalonians 4:15-18; I Corinthians 15:51-57)

   3. Feasts with early and latter rain (Genesis 8:22; Psalm 65:9-13; 107:35-38; Zechariah 10:1; 13:1; Isaiah 55:10; Joel 2:23; James 5:7)

   4. Feasts with a Great Harvest (Exodus 23:14-16; Matthew 13:29-30,36-48; James 5:7; Exodus 34:22)

Acts 2		James 5:7
Early Rain *Former House* Showers that soften the ground for the sowing of seed.	NO RAIN	*Latter Rain* *Latter House* Showers that ripened the fruit for harvest.

IV. THE HARVEST FORETOLD BY THE PROPHETS

A. Prophets and Prophecy
(II Peter 1:19-21; II Timothy 3:15-16; Amos 3:7)

   1. The Nature of Prophecy
      a. Forthtelling
      b. Foretelling (Isaiah 41:22-23; 45:21; 46:9-10)

2. The Historical Fulfillment of Prophecy
3. The National Destiny Scope of Prophecy
4. The Messianic Scope of Prophecy
5. The Last Days Fulfillment or Prophecy

B. Prophets of Harvest
   1. Isaiah 2:1-4
   2. Isaiah 54:1-3; Galatians 4:20-27
   3. Joel 1:10; Joel 2:21-24
   4. Amos 9:11-15; Acts 15:16-18
   5. Isaiah 60:1-9
   6. Isaiah 9:1-7; Matthew 4:14
   7. Isaiah 42:1-10
   8. Ezekiel 17:22-32 inaccurate reference?
   9. Daniel 7:13-14
   10. Hosea 6:11
   11. Malachi 4:6; Matthew 17:12; Mark 9:13
   12. Joel 2:21-32

V. THE HARVEST THEOLOGY OF JESUS
A. Matthew 9:35-37
B. Matthew 13:24-30
C. Matthew 13:31-32
D. Matthew 13:47-52
E. Mark 4:26-29
F. John 4:35-38
G. Acts 1:7-8

VI. THE HARVEST PREDICTED IN BOOK OF REVELATION
A multitude that no man can number from every nation and tribe will be gathered together in the last great harvest, the Harvest of the Feast of Tabernacles. There will be 10 thousand times 10 thousand worshipping the Lamb of God.
A. Revelation 5:9-13; Revelation 7:9-15
B. Revelation 14:6-8; Revelation 14-16
C. Revelation 19:1,6

VII. A HARVEST PHILOSOPHY
A. A philosophy that excites the believer to sharpen their sickle and prepare for the greatest harvest ever reaped in all of history.
B. A philosophy that believes the church is a place of growth, power and excitement; a place that God has ordained to become a force in the earth. God is not pleased with evangelistic or missionary work that does not result in church growth.
C. A philosophy that propagates a positive approach to a negative society; a positive attitude of faith because the answer is found in Christ and Christ is committed to the harvest.

D.   A philosophy of ultimate victory and triumph of the church as God's last instrument to use in His eternal plan and purpose. This plan involves the House being filled with souls from all walks of life.

E.   A philosophy that believes since God as revealed in the Bible has assigned the highest priority to bringing men into living relationship to Jesus Christ, we may define our mission narrowly as an enterprise devoted to proclaiming the Good News of Jesus Christ and to persuading men to become His disciples and dependable members of His church.

F.   A philosophy that sees the world as God's harvest field. Therefore, all unreached people groups in the world must be reached with the Gospel of the Kingdom. A people have been reached only when many of its members have become disciples of Christ and responsible members of His body, till the church is well rooted in that society it has not been reached!

G.   A Harvest philosophy that clearly understands and honestly evaluates all growth by asking these questions: Is it biological growth? Is it transfer growth? Is it conversion growth?

H.   A philosophy that handles the tension of the discipling and perfecting debate. Usually anti-growth attitudes that hinder the harvesting vision and spirit within the church arise out from confusing perfecting with discipleship. The church exists not for herself but for the world. She always has a two-fold task, winning people to Christ and going on to maturity.

VIII. HARVEST REAPED: 21st CENTURY CUTTING-EDGE CHURCH

1990'S SOCIETY II Timothy 4:1-2; 3:1-8,13	*21ST CENTURY CUTTING EDGE CHURCH* The Harvesting Church	*1990'S CHURCH GENERAL CONDITION* II Kings 6:5-7 Revelation 3:14-22
1. Fragmented relationships	1. Biblical relationships	1. Learning relationships
2. Confused and changing values	2. Biblical values	2. Struggling with values
3. Mixture of beliefs	3. Biblical roots	3. Shallowness of doctrine
4. Amoral society	4. Biblical lifestyle	4. Holiness crisis
5. Cynical attitude toward God and church	5. Biblical attitudes	5. Cynical attitude nation/sinners
6. Pessimistic about the future	6. Biblical perspective	6. Mixture of pessimism, escapism
7. Success passion	7. Biblical servanthood	7. Success confusion
8. Independent man	8. Biblical balanced authority	8. Fear of using authority
9. Purposeless	9. Biblical mission purpose	9. Maintenance mentality
10. Global smallness	10. Biblical world view	10. Global awakening
11. Hunger after form of supernatural	11. Biblical passion for power	11. Controversy about supernatural
12. Satanism, occult	12. Biblical weapons of war	12. Spiritual satanic harassment

Vision for a City Reaching Church

Jeremiah 30:17; 29:1; Isaiah 26:1

INTRODUCTION: God is raising up a new breed of spiritual leaders who are vanguards who advance ahead into the future, forerunners who stand in the gap. Emerging at the end of one millennium and standing at the beginning of another, they are navigators of a new century. Today there are insightful leaders who see the emerging work of God and, with leadership skills, move people into the future. City-reaching leaders know how to interpret the times, the spiritual climate, the prophetic signs within their own city context. City-reaching is a vision for today's generation of leaders.

I.   THE CHURCH IN THE CITY

A.   God's View/Perspective of the Church in the City
(Matthew 16:16-18)

1.   The Biblical Perspective of Christ's Church (II Cor 8:1; Gal 1:2; Rev 1-3)

a.   We want to acknowledge "the church" in the "city" refers to the whole church. All congregations who are biblically consistent with the New Testament definition of the church make up the church in the Portland/Vancouver area.

b.   Universal Church (Acts 20:28; Ephesians 5:32)
Not national, international, denominational, undenominational, sectarian or non-sectarian. It is one new man, a new thing!

2.   The Focused Perspective (II Corinthians 11:18)

a.   We want to acknowledge the localized church, each individual congregation of believers that have bishops, deacons and saints. Variety of congregations but one church!

b.   Ekklesia = "called out to assemble together", organism, assembly, congregation, the local church

B.   The Proper Perspective of Local Churches in the City
Revelation 1-3 The seven churches of Asia reveal several truths

1.   Each local church has its own divine destiny. (Romans 8:28-29; Lk 19:44)

2.   Each local church has its own unique personality. We are not to compare or judge another church because it is different. We are not to judge anyone.

3.   Each local church has its own dominant distinctives. We are to accept this as a practical outworking of the church vision, the pastoral ministry and to the shaping power of the Holy Spirit.

4.   Each local church has its own God-given vision/mission which is a reflection of their doctrinal/biblical distinctives, own specific church history background, their present leadership. It will be different, not wrong or sub-Bible because it's not like ours, just different.

II.   GOD'S RELATIONSHIP TO THE CITY

A.   God Hears the Cry of the City
(Genesis 18:20-21)

B.   God Weeps Over the City
(Luke 19:41-44)

C.   God Speaks to the City
(Micah 6:9; Proverbs 1:20-21)

D.   God Sends Ministries to Cities
(Jonah 1:2; Luke 9:51-56)

III.   EVALUATING BIBLICAL MODELS OF MINISTRY TO THE CITY

A.   The Nehemiah Model: A Deep Spiritual Burden for the City
(Nehemiah 1:1-4)

B.   The Pauline Model: A Melting of His Spirit for the City
(Acts 17:16)

C.   The Acts Model: A Key for Every City
(Numbers 13:28; Deuteronomy 1:28; Joshua 6:5,20; Hebrews 11:30)

CITY	THE KEY
Sychar, John 4:28-30, 39-42	One convert, personal miracle, one woman
Jerusalem, Acts 1-4	Prayer, supernatural outpouring
Samaria, Acts 8	Philip the Evangelist (preached Christ; miracles; Simon the Sorcerer converted)
Joppa, Acts 9:36-42	Healing of Dorcas, dead raised

CITY	THE KEY
Caesarea, Acts 10	House meeting, outpouring of Spirit
Antioch, Acts 11	Common men preaching, lay ministries
Lystra, Acts 14	Miracle of lame man
Philippi, Acts 16	House meeting, miracle earthquake
Thessalonica, Acts 17	Teaching
Corinth, Acts 18	Demonstration of the Spirit

Acts 17:6 "But when they did not find them, they dragged Jason and some brethren to the rulers of the city, crying out, 'These who have turned the world upside down have come here too.'"

We are world-turners! We put cities right side up!

IV. THE DIVINE KEY FOR PENETRATING TODAY'S CITIES

A. The Corinthian City: A Microcosm of Modern Day Cities
   1. A Port City: a seaman's paradise, drunkard's heaven, virtuous woman's hell
   2. Immoral City: Temple of Aphrodite, 1000 male and female prostitutes
   3. Educational City: arts, sciences, languages
   4. Sports City
   5. Pleasure City
   6. Mixed Race City

B. Corinthian City Promise - Our Promise

> Acts 18:9-10 Now the Lord spoke to Paul in the night by a vision, "Do not be afraid, but speak, and do not keep silent; for I am with you, and no one will attack you to hurt you; for I have many people in this city."

C. Corinthian Key
   (I Corinthians 2:1-2)
   1. Not excellency of speech, intellectual, enticing words
   2. Much trembling, fear, no confidence in the flesh
   3. Came to you in demonstration of the Spirit
   5. Came to you preaching the cross

V. A STRATEGIC PLAN

A. A strategic plan is to maintain a strong local church with a spiritual armory so as to penetrate the spiritual powers "over" or "in" our city.
   (Jeremiah 50:25)

B. A strategic plan is to reap the harvest God would give us from our city/metro area, using every means available or necessary.
   (Matthew 9:35-37)

C. A strategic plan is to mobilize the local church members throughout our city/metro area through small groups structured for penetrating every neighborhood with the love of God.
(Acts 2:37-47)

D. A strategic plan is to penetrate ever pocket or stronghold of darkness by increasing the ministry of intercessory prayer and corporate prayer.
(Ezekiel 22:30-31)

E. A strategic plan is to help restore the inner city by reaching individuals with Christ (families, youth, singles) and establishing them in the church.
(Isaiah 58:12; 61:4)

F. A strategic plan is to oppose moral perversity, homosexuality, pornography, prostitution (all moral sins that violate God's word) by being salt/light and political involvement as is necessary.
(Isaiah 58:19)

G. A strategic plan is to train spiritual leaders through our schools. These will be dynamic leaders in business, work-market and church world.
(Genesis 14:13; Psalm 87:1-7)

H. A strategic plan is to launch more public ministry to our metro area: Operation City, teams for street ministry, music, drama, concerts, downtown ministry, more intensified city ministry.
(Acts 1:1-8)

I. A strategic plan is to go on Christian radio (our worship and teaching), a local television special for Christmas or Easter, or a family teaching prime time program maybe once a year.

VI. CITY-REACH NINE STEP PLAN
(Ezekiel 4:1-3)

A. **City Proclamation:** A unified effort to repent, request and resist according to Daniel 9:4-9, Jeremiah 29:7, Ephesians 6:10-11 and James 5:7, proclaiming a set time to take back city territory that has been under the rule of Satan and move back under the rule of Christ.
   1. Repent (*Daniel 9:4-9*).
   2. Request (*Jeremiah 29:7*).
   3. Resist (*Ephesians 6:10-17; James 5:7*).

B. **City Stake:** Prayer staking the geographical boundaries of our city with proclamation and repentance. The church is identifying with the corporate sins of Portland, repenting, forsaking and publicly apologizing. These sins include racial hostility toward Afro-Americans, Asians and Indians.
(Isaiah 54:1, Psalm 78:54-55, 16:6, 74:17, 147:14; II Samuel 8:3; Malachi 1:4)

C.   **City Intercession:** Recognizing and standing against principalities and powers which lie behind the chronic historical problems in our city through intercessory prayer and releasing the power of revival into every part of our city with measured results as seen in salvation of all peoples.
(Jeremiah 30:17, 50:2-3; Ezekiel 22:30; Revelation 7:1, 15; Deuteronomy 20:8, 32:8; Ephesians 6:12)

D.   **City Walk:** We are developing a prayer walking strategy for every neighborhood, beginning with northeast and southeast Portland and eventually praying over every part in our city and metropolitan area.
(Joshua 1:3-4; Genesis 13:14-17; I Kings 20:28)

E.   **City Kindness:** A conspiracy of kindness to open hearts for the Gospel, to motivate feeding the hungry and helping the homeless with compassion.

F.   **City Prayer Fair:** A fair for the community where practical and spiritual ends meet.

G.   **City Networking:** A strategy to network like-hearted leaders and churches for greater impact through inter-connecting and cross-pollination.

H.   **City Harvesting**: Using all means possible for city and regional harvest, including the Eternity Productions.

I.   **City Cells**: Using small groups geographically to implement all aspects of the vision for our city.

VII.   CITY PASTORS' COVENANT

A.   We covenant together to strategically and systematically build relationship with other city pastors and leaders within our committed leadership group.

B.   We covenant together to make our meeting times together highest priority, faithfully setting aside these times with discipline and consistency.

C.   We covenant together to publicly pray for the pastors and churches in our covenant group with our congregations, thus expressing and encouraging unity in our metro area.

D.   We covenant together to guard one another. We will resist criticism, unfounded accusations, and competitive carnal words or attitudes. We commit to speaking well of one another.

E.   We covenant together to transfer people from one congregation to another with respect and carefulness. We commit to communicating when people change churches if unresolved offenses need to be dealt with.

F.   We covenant together toward racial reconciliation with biblical respect and love for all races, promoting love, understanding and a continual transparency in the racial issues.

G.   We covenant together to be accountable to this committed group (all individuals within the group). We give permission for confrontation if needed, and questions to be asked, for this group to hold accountable the ethics, standards and practice of being a minister.

H.   We covenant together to pray for the marriages and the children represented in this group. We will strategically seek to strengthen the marriage, home and family.

I.   We covenant together to aggressively intercede for our metro area, taking into consideration our natural and spiritual borders and our responsibility to intercede for government leaders, city officials and city issues.

J.   We covenant together to strategize on how we can better reach our city for Christ. We will work together, help one another and seek to penetrate our metro area.

VIII.   CITY PASTORS' ACTIVITIES

A.   All City Pastors and Leaders Breakfast: A quarterly meeting with a broad, generalized intention of nurturing city unity. We pray for all new church plants and pastors in need. There is a time of worship and usually some speaking.

B.   Monthly Pastors and Leaders Meeting: A deeper commitment group with a specific purpose in mind – relationship, accountability, vision sharing, issues discussion, personal prayer ministry over different pastors each time and intercessory prayer for our region.

C.   Annual Retreat: Designed for both husband and wife to deepen relationships through prayer, word ministry, an outside speaker along with inside speakers.

D.   Church Administrator's Group: Designed to strengthen the church administrators by a monthly gathering. This is well structured with resources, discussion and trouble-shooting.

E.   Youth Pastors and Leaders Groups: Available for those pastors who desire their youth pastors to have relationship and resources on an on-going basis.

F.   First Sunday of the Year City Communion Service: An event for pastors and churches to come together in unity for worship and prayer. City pastors participate in all aspects of the meeting and an offering is taken to dispense to the poor of the city.

G.   All Church Leadership Team Equipping Day: For lay pastors, staff pastors, all main leaders, elders, staff ministry from city churches, a one-day event for strengthening church leaders.

H.   Senior Pastors Wives Luncheon: This is a time of building relationships between the pastor's wives. There is a time of sharing and personal prayer ministry.

I.   All City Churches Prayer Together: A networking of all City Pastors prayer groups for prayer, unity and evangelism.

J.   Community service to the City: Service to the poor, the abused, the orphan, and the widow.

Vision for a World Reaching Church

Revelation 7:9-10; Acts 1:8; Matthew 28:19-20

Introduction: Every local church must cultivate a vision for reaching the nations of the world. Today, in the year 2001, there are 1.6 billion people who have never heard the gospel. That is 27% of the world's population. There are 16,000 languages that have no scripture, no native pastor and no church to attend. Ninety-five percent of the world's pastors minister to 5% of the world's population. Only 9% of the world speaks English and 96% of the church's income is spent among that 9%. There are 37,000 Protestant missionaries from the United States and Canada scattered over the world. They come from 620 mission agencies and churches working in 182 countries.

God is a world person. Oswald J. Smith pastored a church in Toronto, Canada which has contributed 23 million do missions since 1928. He said, "The supreme task of the church is the evangelization of the world. When God loved, He loved a world. When He gave His Son, He gave His Son for a world. When Jesus Christ died, He died for a world. God's vision is a world vision. That is the vision He wants us to have."

As world Christians we must have an attitude that links our small circle of activity to the global community, an attitude that reminds us that our Christian faith rises above cultures and knows neither national boundaries nor ethnic limitations.

I.   WORLD CHURCH VISION

A.   **An international, multi-ethnic church**. We should desire to reach the nations of the world, realizing that the nations are literally here at our door. We must build a bridge of love and trust to the people groups of our cities, targeting different areas and peoples, reaching out and building relationships, gathering them in ethnic fellowships, and welcoming them into the family as one church. *"... no longer foreigners and aliens, but fellow citizens with God's people and members of God's household"*

1.   A multi-ethnic church is a testimony to the city and to the world of the reconciling power of the Holy Spirit.

2.   A multi-ethnic church gives opportunity to all ethnic groups to maintain their own cultural distinctives without being separated from the rest of the Body of Christ. It helps them to keep from being ingrown and self-serving. This becomes increasingly important in the second and third generations.

3.   A multi-ethnic church helps newly arrived people from another ethnic background to more comfortably bridge the gap to further involvement in City Bible Church while in a familiar language and culture environment.

4.   A multi-ethnic church gives opportunity for those with a different ethnic background to gain practical experience and training more quickly in the area of church leadership.

5.   A multi-ethnic church gives an opportunity to all Christians to understand and be united with groups who have a different culture from their own. We learn from one another because of the resulting world perspective.

6. A multi-ethnic church gives the opportunity for ethnic groups to be an arm of City Bible Church to reach out to the various communities throughout the Portland area and back to the home countries represented.

B. **A world vision church.** *"Therefore go and make disciples of all nations...baptizing...teaching them to obey everything I have commanded..."* There are 239 nations and 350 large world-cities that need apostolic churches. Have a world faith for a world vision! We by ourselves can't do this, but we can partner with the Body of Christ, mark our cities and do our share.

C. **A bridge building church.** A bridge provides passage over some type of obstacle: a river, a valley, a road or a set of railroad tracks. The type of bridge used depends on various features of the obstacle. The main feature that controls the type of bridge is the size of the obstacle. There are three major types of bridges, the difference between them being the distance they can reach across: beam bridge, arch bridge and suspension bridge.

D. **A Great Commission church.** This vision is vital to any healthy local church. From the outset it provides a sense of purpose and direction for the people of God. The Holy Spirit desires that we learn to think globally and eternally.

E. **Sample Vision Statement**
Ephesians 3:20 Now to Him who is able to do exceedingly abundantly above all that we ask or think, according to the power that works in us,

1. **Exalting the Lord** by dynamic, Holy Spirit inspired worship, praise and prayer. Giving our time, talents and gifts as an offering to the Lord.
2. **Equipping the church** to fulfill her destiny through godly vision, biblical teaching and pastoral ministries, bringing believers to maturity in Christ and effective ministry, resulting in a restored triumphant church.
3. **Extending the Kingdom** of God through the church, to our city, our nation and the world through aggressive evangelism, training leaders, planting churches and sending missionaries and mission teams.

II. THE GREAT COMMISSION SCRIPTURES AND COMPONENTS

A. The Lesser Commission – Pre-resurrection
(Matthew 10:1,5; Luke 9:1-6; 10:1-20)

B. The Great Commission – Post-resurrection
1. Matthew's Gospel Great Commission: The Specific Task (Mt 28:16-20)
2. Mark's Gospel Great Commission: The Divine Authority (Mark 16:15-16)
3. Luke's Gospel Great Commission: The Crucial Message (Luke 24:44-49)
4. John's Gospel Great Commission: The Awesome Analogy (John 20:21-23)

Summary Statement: The primary mission of the church is to proclaim the gospel of Christ and gather believers into local churches where they can be built up in the faith and made effective in service, thereby planting new congregations throughout the world.

5. The Book of Acts Great Commission (Acts 1:8)

Acts 1:8 has been called "The Great Prophecy." "The context of the final reference to the Great Commission in the post-resurrection ministry of Jesus is portrayed in Acts 1 as the culmination of His instruction in 'the things pertaining to the Kingdom of God' (1:3)... In one brief statement Jesus shows that the coming (baptism) of the Holy Spirit (1:5,8) will so empower His disciples that they will individually and collectively become His bold witnesses. They will begin their witness in Jerusalem and eventually reach outward 'to the end of the earth.' Down through the centuries concerned Christians have seen that God's redemptive purpose must not be thwarted by contentment with past successes. The gospel must go outward and onward in ever widening circles from Jerusalem. To them mission meant both plan and progress. And the singling out of Samaria can only mean God's peculiar concern for minority peoples, the sort that majority peoples tend to despise. Indeed, over the years God has singularly blessed those servants of His who have reminded the Church of the world's 'forgotten peoples' (I Cor 1:26-29)."

C. Great Commission Components

1. The Authority Component (Matthew 28:18; Daniel 7:13-14; Romans 8:28)

2. The Invasion Mandate Component (Matthew 28:19; Luke 19:10)

3. The Discipling Nations Component (Matthew 28:19; 1:1; Genesis 12:3; Matthew 13:10-13)

4. The Kingdom Power Component (Mark 16:17-20; Luke 10:19)

5. The Systematic Training Component (Matthew 28:20; II Timothy 2:7)

6. The Divine Empowerment Component (Matthew 28:20; Genesis 28:15; Judges 6:12; Acts 18:10; John 14:23; Mark 16:18; Luke 10:19)

III. THE GREAT COMMISSION CHRISTIAN

A. A Great Commission Christian receives supernatural power
"You shall receive power" (Matthew 7:8; 10:8; 13:20-21; Mark 11:24; John 1:12; 1:16; 7:39; 20:22; Acts 2:38)

B. A Great Commission Christian is clothed with the Holy Spirit
"When the Holy Spirit comes upon you" (Luke 1:35; 11:22; Acts 1:8; 8:24)

C. A Great Commission Christian bears witness by his death.
"Shall be witnesses to me" (Luke 24:46-49; Acts 5:32; 13:30-31; 22:15)

D. A Great Commission Christian begins in their city.
"Jerusalem"

E.   A Great Commission Christian takes responsibility for their region.
       "Judea"

F.   A Great Commission Christian reaches out to all people groups
       "Samaria" (Acts 17:26; 10:34; Genesis 12:3; 1:26; Matthew 24:14; 28:19; Mark
       11:17; Luke 24:46-47; Acts 2:5; 17:24-27; Galatians 3:8; Revelation 5:9)

G.   A Great Commission Christian embraces a global vision.
       "Ends of the earth" (Acts 1:8; 13:47)

H.   A Great Commission Christian gives faithfully, sacrificially and strategically.
       (Deuteronomy 14:22-23; Nehemiah 10:37-39; Proverbs 3:9-10; I Kings 17:7-16;
       Luke 6:38; Genesis 14:17-24; I Chronicles 29:14-18)

IV.   GREAT RESPONSE TO A GREAT COMMISSION
(Hebrews 3:7)

A.   A Personal Response
       (Isaiah 6:1-10; Romans 1:14-15; Acts 26:19-20)

       Luasanne Covenant: "World evangelization requires the whole church to take the
       whole gospel to the whole world"

B.   A Corporate Response
       (Luke 12:48; Psalm 2:8)
       1.   A commitment to becoming a Great Commission church
       2.   A commitment to developing Holy Spirit-inspired strategies to reach our
              world
       3.   A commitment to intercessory prayer for "all nations" of the world
       4.   A commitment to sacrificial giving of our best leaders to missions work
       5.   A commitment to sacrificial giving of our money, now, today for missions
              (Matthew 6:19-21)

Vision for a Church Planting Church

Acts 16:9; Luke 6:38; Matthew 28:18-20; Matthew 9:37-38; Acts 1:7-8

Introduction: Everything that God designs reproduces. We see this in nature and in the creation of man: reproduce, multiply, fill the whole earth. Church planting should be given a central position in strategies for city and world evangelization. Church planting is biblical; it is the model shown us in the New Testament for extending the Kingdom of God. The vision to plant new churches must be in the vision of the overseeing leadership of the local church and a strategy in uniting to fulfill this vision.

> The primary mission of the church and therefore of the churches is to proclaim the Gospel of Christ and gather believers into local churches where they can be built up in the faith and made effective in service, thereby planting new congregations throughout the world.

I. CHURCH PLANTING AND THE CHURCH PLANTER
(I Corinthians 3:10)

A. The church planter must be prepared practically, personally and spiritually.

B. The church planter must be sent by the local church

C. The church planter must be covered in prayer before, during and after.

D. The church planter must have patience and a teachable spirit.

E. The church planter must expect delays, misunderstanding, loneliness, financial challenges

II. CHURCH PLANTING AND CHURCH PLANT TEAMS

A. Church planting needs to be done by teams not just a pastor alone.

B. Church plant teams need to be chosen carefully.

C. Church plant teams need a unified vision.

D. Church plant teams need a unified ministry philosophy.

III. CHURCH PLANTING MODELS

A. The church plant by a local church by sending a church planter without a team.

B. The church plant by a local church by sending a church planter with a team.

C. The church plant by a local church within the same geographical area.

D. The church plant by a local church outside the geographical area.

E. The church plant not sent by the local church but adopted by the local church.

F. The church plant that is unplanned and unwanted but turns out anyway.

G. The church plant that is a satellite of the mother church.
These are not totally autonomous but could be called branch churches. The satellite church also has different models within this concept

H. The multi-ethnic church within the church congregation's minority groups that functions as a church in the same facility with a overseeing ethnic pastor yet relating to the senior pastor of that local church.

I. The multiple campus church – one church, many locations.
The concept here is that one local congregation led by the same staff, with one membership roll, one budget, one senior pastor and yet with weekly sermons at different locations.

J. The cross-cultural church plant by a sending church.
Sending a leader with or without a team to another people group within or without the geographical area

IV. A Sample of Church Planting Process

A. Candidate meets with their district pastor. If the district pastor feels that the person is a qualified candidate, a church planting questionnaire will be given to the candidate before seeing Pastor Frank.

B. Candidate meets with Pastor Frank for first step approval. The vision is shared and, if Pastor Frank confirms the candidate's vision, he is then sent to the church planting office for processing.

C. Candidate meets with the church planting office. Here the candidate shares his vision and submits approved application.

D. Candidate meets again with the church planting office where his questionnaire is discussed and a preparation plan and checklist is developed for the candidate.

E.   Candidate then submits the preparation plan to Pastor Frank for further development.

F.   Candidate works on the areas of preparation suggested by Pastor Frank and the church planting office. (Note: this could take months or years depending on the previous work of preparation and the ministry maturity of the candidate)

G.   Candidate presents vision to Pastor Frank, then pastor Frank will set in eldership time.

H.   Candidate presents the vision to the elders for their scrutiny, confirmation and approval. If the elders approve, the process continues. If they do not approve, a further process of preparation will be developed for the candidate who moves back into position #E above.

I.   Pastor Frank will then set an official date for the actual sending out of the candidate by the mother church.

J.   Pastor Frank, with the candidate, selects the elders who will serve with him through the church planting process until elders within the new work have been raised up and set in place.

K.   An announcement is made to the congregation regarding the planting of a new church. Members of the mother church who feel inclined to go are encouraged to fast and pray and then meet with their district pastor to discuss their possible involvement in the new work.

L.   As the district pastors affirm the involvement of various "team members", they will be given permission to meet as a team in preparation for the plant.

M.   The candidate will be invited to meet with the elders in all of their meetings until they are actually sent forth.

N.   The team will be given permission to meet for services of their own on Sunday nights four months prior to the plant.

O.   The team will be given permission to meet for services of their own on Sunday mornings two months prior to the plant and they may also begin tithing to the new work at this time.

P.   The candidate will be licensed by the mother church.

Q.   The candidate will file Articles of Incorporation for the new work.

R.   A sending service will be scheduled by Pastor Frank for the church plant where the candidate and the church planting team will be prayed over.

188

Vision for a Church That Grows

Introduction: We are to aggressively reach out and reap the harvest of lost people, unchurched people and prodigals. There is no room for a complacent vision of "let them come to us." We are to go out into the highways and byways and compel them to come in. Our vision is to grow through reaching all people, all races, at all times with the gospel of Christ. We are not to stagnate or allow a passive spirit to hinder us. We are to break out and grow.

I. GROWTH ACTION PLAN

Strategic Leadership	+	Unified Vision	+	Positive Growth Momentum	+	Healthy Leadership District Team	=	Multiplication Level Growth

II. REACHING THE MULTITUDES

A. The First Church Ministered to the Multitudes
(Acts 4:32; 6:2; 6:5; 14:1; 14:4; 15:12; 15:30; 17:4)

B. Seeing the Multitude with Spiritual Eyes
1. Multitudes of people who have multiplied needs (Mk 8:1)
2. Multitudes of people who are in a deserted place
3. Multitudes of people who are like a sheep without a shepherd (Mk 6:34; Mt 9:36-37)
4. Multitudes of people who are hungry with no place to get food
5. Multitudes of people who have deep spiritual bondages and satanic harassment (Mk 3:7-11; Mt 17:14)
6. Multitudes of people who will respond to Jesus with worship (Mt 21:8)
7. Multitudes of people who need spiritual and physical healing (Mk 2:13,17; 5:21-29; 7:33-35; 10:46-52; Lk 6:17-19; Jn 5:3)

III. DISCERNING OUR FAITH LEVEL FOR THE MULTITUDES

A. The John 6:5 Challenge for the Multitudes

B. The Disciples Faith Level

1. The attitude and flawed perspective exposed (Jn 6:5-6)

2. The Philip Attitude: "It's not within our budget and we can't afford the multitudes." (Jn 6:7)

3. The Andrew Attitude: "It's not within our power or our resources. We only have enough for five loaves and two fishes." (Jn 6:8-9)

4. The Twelve Disciples Attitude: "Send them away" (Lk 9:12)

C. The Jesus Faith Level

1. The attitude of We care: compassion for the multitudes of people (Matthew 9:36-37)

2. The attitude of We can: we have everything we need to minister to their needs (Mk 6:6; Mt 14:16)

3. The attitude of We have: we have all the virtue and power needed to touch all

IV. THE JESUS' STRATEGY FOR MINISTERING TO THE MULTITUDES

A. Jesus chooses and uses people as His channels of ministry to the multitudes (Matthew 14:16)

B. Jesus uses our limited resources to minister to the multitudes (Matthew 14:17-18)

C. Jesus manages the multitudes by arranging them in small groups (Matthew 14:19)

D. Jesus desires to use your life to touch the people in groups (Matthew 14:19)

Vision for A Church
Whose Fruit Remains

Introduction: Botanists know exactly what they mean when they talk about fruit. A fruit is the seedbearing organ of a plant or tree. When we pastors speak about fruit, do we know exactly what we mean? How does the local church cultivate an orchard of great spiritual fruit that remains? We are hard at work preparing the soil, planting the seed, weeding, watering, pruning and believing we will have fruit that remains. The vision of every pastor should be to plant a spiritual legacy, a fruit tree that forever keeps bearing fruit. Fruit that remains is a matter of planning, wisdom, and forethought. In this session we will examine our fruit bearing, fruit remaining skills.

John 15:16 Amplified: You have not chosen Me, but I have chosen you and I have appointed you [I have planted you], that you might go and bear fruit and keep on bearing, and that your fruit may be lasting [that it may remain, abide], so that whatever you ask the Father in My Name [as presenting all that I am], He may give it to you.

I.   **THE FRUIT-BEARING LEADER BEFORE A FRUIT-BEARING VINEYARD**
      (John 15:16; Philippians 1:22; Colossians 1:6 and 10; Genesis 1:11-12; Luke 6:43-44)
      We reproduce what we are, "according to its kind."

    A.   Leaders fruit bearing begins with understanding their calling
      (Deuteronomy 7:7-8; Isaiah 48:11)
      "You did not choose me, I chose you."

    B.   Leaders fruit bearing begins with understanding their placement
      "And appointed you"

    C.   Leaders fruit bearing begins with the leaders understanding of abiding
      "Should go and bear fruit"

    D.   Leaders fruit bearing must continue on to become fruit remaining
      "And your fruit should remain"

II.   **THE FRUIT-BEARING VINEYARD**
      (John 15; Isaiah 5:1-5)

> **Leonardo da Vinci, painter of the Mona Lisa, one of history's unmatched inventors and artists said on his deathbed, "I have offended God and mankind because my work does not reach the quality it should have."**[1]

[1]Tommy Barnett. <u>Adventure Yourself</u>. (Lake Mary, FL: Creation House, 2000), p. 57-58.

A.   The "No Fruit" Church: Lifeless branches bear nothing
(Jn 15:4-5; Lk 8:14; 13:6-7)

B.   The "Bad Fruit" Church: The church is producing fruit but it is not usable or healthy fruit.
(Luke 6:43-44)

C.   The "Some Fruit" Church: This church has some life and some fruit but it is not noticeable.
(John 15:2; Romans 1:13; 7:4)

D.   The "More Fruit" Church: This church has been through some seasons of pruning and removing the dead wood and good wood.
(John 15:2)

E.   The "Much More Fruit" Church: This church is practicing all the fruit-bearing principles in a systematic way so as to have consistent, abundant fruit.
(John 15:5; 15:8; Mark 4:20)

F.   The "Fruit Remaining" Church: This church has learned the secret of keeping the fruit year after year, generation after generation.
(John 15:16; Luke 8:15; Romans 15:28)

III.   THE CAUSES OF POOR YIELDS

A.   Fruit is damaged or diseased
(Mk 4:5-6; Ex 10:15; Mt 3:10; 7:19; 21:19)

B.   Fruit is treated with impatience
(James 5:7)

C.   Fruit vines have poor pruning
(John 15:2; Leviticus 25:3; Hebrews 12:11)

D.   Fruit is carelessly picked

E.   Fruit is left unattended
(Psalm 80:12; Mark 4:7; Proverbs 24:30-34)

IV. REJUVENATING NEGLECTED TREES
(Proverbs 24:30)

A. Diagnosing the damaged tree problems.

B. Rejuvenating Principles

V. A VINEYARD WHOSE FRUIT REMAINS
(John 15:16 Amplified)

A. A vineyard planted in good soil and by good water.
(Ezek 17:8; Ps 1:3; Jer 17:8; Rev 22:2)

B. A vineyard planted with the right seed
(Deuteronomy 22:9)

C. A vineyard pruned consistently and wisely
(Lev 25:3-4; Is 5:6; John 15:6)

D. A vineyard protected from external and internal dangers
(Isaiah 5:5; Matthew 21:33; Isaiah 5:2; Song of Solomon 2:15; Psalm 80:12-13)

Vision for the Mystery of the Seed

Genesis 8:22 "Seedtime and harvest"

INTRODUCTION: Seeds are one of nature's mighty miracles for in a seed lies the fierce force of life. Often used as a symbol of a beginning, seeds are living guarantees of continuity between generations. Inside the most minute, dust-like grain of seed is a living plant. This seed will go through stages of development not discerned by naked eyes, but it lives. A vision leader is called to spiritual gardening or farming. The leader is given seeds to sow, to nurture and to bring to fruitfulness. All leaders must have a vision for handling spiritual seed and for enhancing their ability to bring the seed to full maturity.

I.   **THE MYSTERY AND MIRACLE OF SEEDS**
      (Genesis 47:19; Psalm 126:6)

    A.   Defining the Seed
        1.   Hebrew: *Zera*, the Hebrew word for seed is used 228 times in the Old Testament and is translated seed, sowing, seedtime, harvest, offspring, descendants.
        2.   Dictionary: That from which anything springs, the first principle of the original, that which contains life, to grow to maturity under right conditions.

    B.   Miracle of Seeds
        (Genesis 1:11,12,29)

    C.   The Significance of Seeds Biblically
        (Matthew 13:19-38; 17:20; Luke 8:11; II Corinthians 9:10; I Peter 1:23; I John 3:9; I Corinthians 15:35)

II.   **SEED SOWING BASICS**
      (Mark 4:26-27; Galatians 6:7-8; Haggai 2:19)

    A.   The Timing

    B.   The Right Soil
        (Ezekiel 17:5; Numbers 20:5)

    C.   The Right Depth

    D.   The Right Seed
        (Jeremiah 2:21)

III. **THE FOUR LOCKS IN EVERY SEED**
      (Leviticus 26:16; Zechariah 8:12)

Seeds have an intricate mechanism which determines the right time and the right place for sprouting. A seed must be absolutely sure it has arrived at a certain safe and suitable place. All four locks must be opened. If three conditions are met but not the fourth, the seed will not grow. A seed only fails if these locks are not opened properly.

A. The Water Lock

B. The Oxygen Lock

C. The Temperature Lock

D. The Light Lock

IV. THE DELAYED GERMINATION FACTOR

A. Seed may be Unfilled.

B. Seed may be in a Dormancy Stage.

C. Seed may be in a Seed Lock.

V. THE SEEDSMAN AND THE PRECIOUS SEED
(Psalm 106:27; Genesis 47:19)

A. A seedsperson is a person who handles seeds, a sower and reaper. He knows the seed timing and the seed unlocking mechanisms.

B. A seedsperson does not plant good seed ideas in bad soil.

C. The seedsperson sows the seed wisely and liberally with faith in the power of the seed. The seedsperson sows the seed of:
(James 5:7-8)
   1. Sowing the seed of faith, expecting supernatural results (Matthew 17:20)
   2. Sowing the seed of the word, expecting God's promises to work (Matthew 24:14; Luke 8:11; I Peter 1:24)
   3. Sowing the seed of finance, expecting a harvest to be reaped (II Corinthians 9:6-10)
   4. Sowing the seed of the gospel, expecting people to be born again (I Peter 1:23; I John 3:9; Revelation 14:14-16; 11:15; 17:14)
   5. Sowing the seed of the kingdom, with a belief in God's sovereignty (Mark 4:26-28; I Corinthians 3:6; John 3:8; Acts 12:10)
   6. Sowing the seed of spiritual principle, expecting spiritual results (Galatians 6:7-8).
   7. Sowing a small, insignificant seed expecting great significant results (Mark 4:30-32; Revelation 7:9; Isaiah 53:3; Daniel 2:35).

VI. THE GROWTH OF SUPERNATURAL SEEDS IS

A. Imperceptible

B. Constant

C. Inevitable

D. Slow but sure

E. God's plan

Vision Renewed Through Prayer and Fasting

INTRODUCTION: As the people of God mature in fulfilling their God-given vision, there must be times set aside to renew faith and the spirit of the vision. This time in the Old Testament was called the Solemn Assembly, a time to hear God's voice fresh and new, to repent and change the heart and mind. This was a time to refocus our eyes on God's purposes. Every church vision warrants a Solemn Assembly time. (Joel 1:14; 2:15)

I.   **DISCERNING THE TRUMPET SOUND: Message Sent From God**
     (Joel 2:15)

     A.   The Different Trumpet Signals
          (Numbers 10:1-10)

         1.   Trumpet to signal congregational gathering (Numbers 10:3)
          2.   Trumpet to signal leaders to gather (Numbers 10:4)
          3.   Trumpet to signal advance of the camp (Numbers 10:5)
          4.   Trumpet to signal alarm, prepare for war (Numbers 10:8-9)
          5.   Trumpet to sound over the beginnings of months and over the offerings
               (Numbers 10:10)

     B.   The Trumpets Were Blown by the Priests
          (Numbers 10:1-4)

     C.   The Trumpets Were to Be Understood Clearly by the People
          (I Corinthians 14:7-8)

     D.   The Trumpet Blown in Zion
          (Hebrews 12:22-26; 12:19)

II. **DRAWING THE CONGREGATION TOGETHER FOR DIVINE PURPOSE**
     (Joel 2:15-16; Numbers 10:3; Leviticus 23:26; Numbers 29:35; Deuteronomy 16:8)

     A.   Solemn assembly is a total, all congregational gathering
          (Leviticus 8:3; Numbers 8:9; II Chronicles 20:13)

     B.   The comprehensiveness of the call underscores the urgency of the need.
          1.   Sanctify the whole congregation
          2.   Assemble the elders
          3.   Gather the children and nursing babes
          4.   Bridegroom and bride

III.   SOLEMN ASSEMBLY IS A TIME FOR FASTING AND SPECIALIZED PRAYING

A.   United Fasting and Prayer
(Joel 2:12-17; 1:14)

1.   Scripture reveals a personalized, individualized fasting and a corporate fasting.

2.   Matthew 18:18-20 When two agree and come together...
a.   Chrysostom (400 AD): "What we cannot obtain by solitary prayer we may by united prayer because when our individual strength fails, there union and concord are effectual."
b.   Thomas Payne: "...Glorious fact that the prayers of a sanctified host, when of one heart and soul become irresistible."
c.   Charles Finney: "Nothing tends more to cement the hearts of Christians than praying together. Never do they love one another so well as when they witness the outpouring of each other's hearts in prayer."

B.   Fasting and Prayer: Partners in Power

One of the most effective ways to increase your spiritual alertness is to combine prayer and fasting. Fasting and prayer is one of the most powerful weapons the Lord has given to the Christian. While practiced by few, nevertheless, prayer – joined with fasting – has been a spiritual discipline used by God to increase spiritual alertness, desire and effectiveness. Fasting can be defined as voluntary abstinence from food for the purpose of concentrated prayer. Consider the following quotes:

- Paul Yonggi Cho: Being full of the Holy Spirit does not necessarily cause one to walk in the power of the Spirit. I believe the way into power...is to fast and pray.
- Keil and Delitzch: "The early church called a fast *statio* because he who fasted had to wait in prayer day and night like a soldier at his post."
- Andrew Murray: "Faith needs a life of prayer in which to grow and keep strong. Prayer needs fasting for its full and perfect development. It is only in a life of moderation and temperance and self-denial that there will be the heart or the strength to pray much. We are creatures of the senses: fasting helps to express, to deepen and to confirm the resolution that we are ready to sacrifice anything, to sacrifice ourselves, to attain what we seek for the Kingdom of God."
- Franklin Hall: "If fasting was practiced in the churches today to the extent it is practiced in the Orient and among heathen, there is every indication that the church of Jesus Christ would be blessed with major signs, healings and miracles all of the time instead of just a sprinkling here and there."
- Bill Gothard: "Our ability to perceive God's direction is directly related to our ability to sense the inner promptings of His Holy Spirit. God provides a specific activity to assist us in doing this – fasting."
- Leonard Ravenhill: "Prayer is a battle for full-grown men, fully armed and fully awake to the possibilities of grace."

C.   Fasting in Judaism

1. There was one official fast given by Yahweh (Day of Atonement).
2. After the Babylonian captivity, the pious Jews established a twice weekly fast (Monday and Thursday) which soon turned into a dead ritual.
3. The Gentiles recognized fasting as a mark of a Jew.
4. After the destruction of the Temple in 70 AD, fasting more or less replaced sacrifice for the Jew.

D. Fasting in Church History

Church history records the establishing of certain days as days of fasting shortly after the first century. Many church fathers emphasized fasting and practiced it in their own lives, but it eventually became a dead ritual, the form without the power, as it did in Judaism.

1. Wednesdays and Fridays became regular fast days as did the "Easter" fast and the fast of Lent.
2. Baptismal candidates and those baptizing also were required to fast before the baptismal service.
3. Polycarp (110 AD) said fasting was a powerful aid against temptation and fleshly lusts.
4. Tertullian (210 AD) said fasting was an aid in controlling passions.
5. Martin Luther not only maintained the spiritual discipline of fasting one day each week, but additionally fasted so often along with his three hours of daily prayer that he was often criticized for fasting too much.
6. Calvin said that fasting should be used as a restraint on the flesh or as a preparation for prayer or as a testimony of our humiliation before God.
7. John Knox impacted the whole of Britain and moved the world toward God as he wrestled day and night in prayer and fasted regularly.
8. Wesley required all ministers to promise to fast. He required all Methodists to fast Wednesday and Fridays until about four in the afternoon.
9. Charles G. Finney, probably the greatest and most anointed soul-winner since the Apostle Paul, fasted every week. Whenever he sensed the work of God slowing down or less of the power of God on his ministry, he would spend another two or three days in fasting and prayer and he testified that the power was always restored.
10. Azusa Street revival came as a result of a ten day time of prayer and fasting (1906), as did every other revival in Christian history.

IV. THE POWER OF FASTING

A. Biblical Purposes
1. Facing impossible circumstances (Nehemiah 1:4; I Samuel 31:13)
2. For repentance (cleansing) (I Samuel 7:6; Nehemiah 9:1; Jonah 3:5)
3. To hear from God (fresh direction) (Ezra 8:21)
4. To provoke God to move on their behalf (II Chronicles 20:3; Esther 4:16; Daniel 9:3; Job 23:3-5; Isaiah 41:21)
5. To petition the Lord (spiritual breakthrough) (Hebrews 5:7; Acts 10:30)

6.   To seek the mind of God (Acts 13:2; 14:23)
7.   To prepare for ministering the power and grace of God (Matt 4:2; Acts 13:3)
8.   For spiritual power (Matthew 17:21; Luke 4:14)
9.   To afflict the soul (Leviticus 16:29; Psalm 35:13; Proverbs 20:27; I Thessalonians 5:23; Hebrews 4:12)
10.   To break the stronghold of the appetite

    B.   Conclusion

1. Watch your motive
a. It is not a way to earn God's blessing and God's answer to your prayer.
b. It is not a way to by-pass obedience.
c. It is not an automatic way to a miracle.
d. It does not accumulate power to your credit so you can display it at will.
2. Fasting is one of the three foundational pillars of the faith (Matthew 6:1-18 – Giving, praying, fasting), and releases the power of God into our lives, bringing a fresh word from Him, as well as deliverances, healings, answers to prayer, victories over temptations, fortification of the spirit, and putting the soul and body in place. Authors and speakers are continually saying that fasting and prayer are the most effective means of achieving this inner strength. My prayer is that God will birth this truth in our church, and that in turn we may reap the spiritual benefits.

    C.   Final Thoughts on Fasting
       1.   Fasting deepens humility.
       2.   Fasting can deepen hunger for God to work.
       3.   Fasting intensifies prayer concentration.
       4.   Fasting solidifies determination.
       5.   Fasting feeds your faith.
       6.   Fasting opens you more fully to the Spirit's working.
       7.   Fasting fires earnestness and zeal.

    D.   Practical Suggestions
       1.   Fast for a meal occasionally and spend the mealtime (and, if possible, additional time) in prayer.
       2.   Pray about planning for fasting as a regular part of your devotional life.
       3.   Spend the first part of your time feasting on God's word, worshipping, adoring and praising the Lord.
       4.   Be flexible in your fasting. Set a fasting goal rather than being legalistic.
       5.   Do not attempt long fasts (20-40 days) unless you have been informed how to do it.
       6.   Keep a listening ear for the Lord's guidance when He calls you to a special fast for a particular need.
       7.   Keep your fasting a matter between you and God alone.

Vision Implementation

Introduction: Implementation is the practical side of vision which leaders may neglect, thinking vision will come about God's way without their help. God always uses men and women – and their free will choices – to bring about fulfillment of vision. Without the implementation of vision, the vision remains in the heavenlies forever. Implementation is the practical working out of the vision. Implementation is the art of taking vision from the imagination stage to the realization stage with wisdom, smoothness and biblical accuracy – with minimum misjudgments which could damage vision momentum.

I.   **COMMON PITFALLS WHEN IMPLEMENTING THE VISION**

      A.   The Pitfall of Presumptuous Vision
(Exodus 18:11; 21:14; Deuteronomy 1:43; 17:12-13; 18:20; Nehemiah 9:10,16,29; Psalm 19:12-13)

            1.   If your vision is presumptuous, meaning it is doing what you want to do rather than what God wants to do, then it will ultimately fail. Also, some pastors have a vision which is beyond their gifting and/or capabilities. Some pastors have an enormous vision but for the wrong motives, often to boost their self-esteem.

            2.   Presumption is doing what you want to do; faith is doing what God says. Presumption is a form of pride. A presumptuous person assumes too much in his favor, especially in the area of authority.

            3.   We must humble ourselves by recognizing our limitations and remaining within our personal ministerial capacity. (Exodus 18:21)

      B.   The Pitfall of Changing Course Hastily
Change comes slowly and the wise leader will nurture his flock through change. Hastiness, rashness and quick decisions without preparing the flock will hinder the pastor's relationship and leadership. (Proverbs 20:21; 21:5; 29:20)

      C.   The Pitfall of Mismanagement of Vision
A vision must be managed. There is a difference between a manager and a visionary. Visionaries are often not given to detail. They can see the long-range goal, but may not give attention to the details of how to get to the goal, or may not need to get bogged down in the details necessary for managing the vision. Someone has to be a detail person. Either the visionary must find the balance between vision and management or he must delegate it to someone else.

Comparison of Leaders and Managers	
Leaders Tend To...	*Managers Tend To...*
Stress relationships with others, values and commitments, the emotional spiritual aspects of the organization	Stress organization, coordination, and control of resources
Create and articulate a vision of what the organization could achieve in the long run	Focus on achieving short-term objectives and goals
Move the organization in new directions, being unsatisfied with the status quo	Concentrate on maximizing results from existing functions and systems
Favor taking risks	Fear uncertainty and act cautiously

Secrets of Effective Leadership, by F.A. Manske, Jr.

D. The Pitfall of Pride
Some pastors are too proud to ask for help. It's important to allow and even invite others with proven ministries to come and critique your church, your ministry, your weaknesses. A good leader is constantly taking inventory as to the effectiveness of his ministry and asking the question, "How can we do it better?" (Proverbs 16:18)

E. The Pitfall of Work Overload

1. The tendency for man pastors is to everything themselves. We tend to think that nobody can do it as good as us! The effective pastor must learn to delegate!

2. Key principles of delegation
   a. Make the instructions, goals and *parameters* clear.
   b. Give the person the authority and the resources.
   c. Give the person the continued support.
   d. Give the person a time to report on the progress.
   e. Give the person recognition when the task is completed.

II. **COMMON CONGREGATIONAL PITFALLS**
(Joshua 1-6)

A. The Pitfall of Wrong Local Church Concepts
(Joshua 1:7-8)

B. The Pitfall of Wrong Kingdom of God Concepts
(Joshua 2:9,11; 3:10,13)

C. The Pitfall of Apathy and Selfishness
(Joshua 4:1–5:15)

D.   The Pitfall of Past Hurts
       (Joshua 6-12)

E.   The Pitfall of Unbelief

F.   The Pitfall of Compromise

III.   THE IMPORTANT FACTORS OF IMPLEMENTATION
Implementing the vision is both an art and a science. While we certainly believe in practicing the spiritual dynamics of church planting and building, nevertheless there are common sense practices that some pastors may feel "too spiritual" to recognize and apply. The church is an organization as well as an organism. There are certain truths which are helpful to understand and apply *organizationally* when it comes to implementing the vision.

A.   Organization Factor

      • Staffing   • Principles of management
      • Leadership style   • Finances
      • Speaking skills   • Sociological factors
      • Demographics   • Human development factors
      • Study skills   • Practices that are proven to be time-wasters and failures

B.   The Light Factor
       (Ps 43:3; Is 50:10-11; Eph 3:17-18; I Pet 2:9; Hb 11:8; Gen 1:1-3; Col 1:13; I Cor 13:12)

C.   The Truth Factor
       (Psalm 43:3; II Peter 1:12; Matthew 4:4)

D.   The Communication Factor
       (Habakkuk 2:1-7)

E.   The Structure Factor

F.   The Balance Factor

G.   The Strategy Factor

H.   The Prophetic Factor

I.   The Equipping Factor
       (Ephesians 4:11-16; Matthew 28:19-20)

> One definition of leadership is the ability to recognize the special abilities
> and limitations of others, combined with the capacity to fit each
> one into the job where he will do his best.

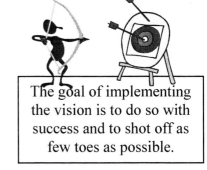

The goal of implementing the vision is to do so with success and to shot off as few toes as possible.

J.   The Timing Factor
(Joshua 3:1-10; Exodus 2:11-17,23-25; Exodus 3:1-9)

K.   The Wise Transition Factor
(Isaiah 2:3; 40:27-31)

L.   The Pacing Factor
(Genesis 33:13-14; Acts 27:7)

M.   The Team Staffing Factor
(Matthew 11:29-30; II Corinthians 6:14; Philippians 4:3; Matthew 19:6; I Corinthians 1:10; 3:9; II Corinthians 6:1,14)

IV.   STRATEGY AND WISE IMPLEMENTATION

A.   Spiritual Ingredients for Vision Implementation
    1.   Corporate unity (Joshua 1)
    2.   Courageous faith (Joshua 2)
    3.   Commitment to godly leadership (Joshua 3)
    4.   Congregation that sacrifices (Joshua 4-5)
    5.   Conquest strategy with a warrior's spirit (Joshua 6)

It All Comes Down To A:

Point of Action
Step of Faith
Power of God
Godly Determination
Godly Commitment

B.   Practical Ingredients
    1.   Wise decision making
    2.   Wise planning
    3.   Financial resources
    4.   Sufficient facilities
    5.   Strong, simple structure
    6.   Balanced staffing